SOPHIA

SOPHIA

Christopher Greaves

AuthorHouse™ UK Ltd.
1663 Liberty Drive
Bloomington, IN 47403 USA
www.authorhouse.co.uk
Phone: 0800.197.4150

© 2013 Christopher Greaves. All rights reserved.

No part of this book may be reproduced, stored in a retrieval system, or transmitted by any means without the written permission of the author.

Published by AuthorHouse   06/25/2013

ISBN: 978-1-4817-9848-8 (sc)
ISBN: 978-1-4817-9849-5 (e)

Any people depicted in stock imagery provided by Thinkstock are models, and such images are being used for illustrative purposes only.
Certain stock imagery © Thinkstock.

Because of the dynamic nature of the Internet, any web addresses or links contained in this book may have changed since publication and may no longer be valid. The views expressed in this work are solely those of the author and do not necessarily reflect the views of the publisher, and the publisher hereby disclaims any responsibility for them.

My thanks to Maria Ross, Lucia Borghi

and Maria-Rosa Apostolo.

Also, as ever, to Steve Kirby and to Ruth.

FOREWORD

The story of Lord Jesus can be likened to a *raga*. We know its overall form well enough, yet its style, its mood and emphases will vary each time it is told. And as with a *raga*, its rendition should be poetic. It should, if possible, be lyrical. Otherwise, if his story is merely told prosaically, the result will also be prosaic. That is: if we say that Christ was someone about whom certain claims are made, who lived at such and such a time, who according to the records did this and that, who is believed by some to be so and so, etcetera, etcetera—we will have entered that realm of frigid academic rationality where nothing is true and all concepts are under erasure. But if we wish to tell the tale of Christ as something that has *meaning*, that can move us or even transform us, then our performance should have an intense, articulate, melodic quality—or it should aim at that, at least.

What follows is one such performance. And in attempting this raga of Christ, I would like to present an imagined arrangement of John's—that is, an orderly, passionate and rhythmical exposition that might have been composed by the disciple John when, in his very old age, he looked back on the teachings of Jesus, on what had become of them, and on what he conceived to be their essence.

THE WELL

There is a well in my garden whose water is sweet and refreshing, yet few are those who care to drink from it. They have sources of their own with which they are content, though to the palate their water is stale and in summer unwholesome. Still, they are used to it. It is what their parents drank, it is what their parents' parents drank, it is all they know.

I tell my neighbours of the water in my well, how sweet it is, how it quenches the thirst, but with a shake of the head or a smile they turn aside. I see how they regard me: as an old man lost in memory, speaking old men's words and thinking old men's thoughts.

And it is true: it is dusk or later in the life of my body. Infirm, my hair grown white, my burned skin sore, I lean where I used to stand and stumble where I used to walk. On the Lord's day young men of our faith come to bear me on a litter into Ephesus, to the church of our Mother, for prayer and thanksgiving. In mirrors, in silver, in water, I catch sight of my face and think, 'Surely that is the face of a stranger'. It is lined and worn and alien. It is something I wear, like the face I had when I was born. Then it was as a mask, inexpressive, but I learned to use it and grew into it and took the part of it; now again it turns into a mask. When I see it I think: I am not this, nor is this I.

Yes, it is true: night falls in the life of my body, the sea's voice murmurs, the last birds sing. Night falls and the fishing boats rest at anchor, their day's catch stored. Night falls upon Ephesus as, over there in the distance, a band of men return towards the citadel. They are tired, their horses kick up dust, they hardly hear the night-birds in the olive trees, they hardly see the stars blaze forth and hardly know their horses kick up dust like incense—for their thoughts are turned toward their homes as they stare down the blackening road, their long work done. Night falls as though from nowhere, imperceptibly yet ceaselessly, and in the life of my body it is also now late and dark.

But there are things that I still wish to say that they might be remembered, before night falls entirely and I discard this mask forever: things concerning Jesus and his mother Mary—and the one who came later, Paul.

THE VISITORS

Some, of course, still come to see me. From far and very far they come: from Antioch and Rome, from the little towns of Syria, from Egypt, from Gaul, Germania, Britannia. They come because I am John, John of Patmos, the Evangelist, the last of Christ's apostles. But how many come out of curiosity, because I am the only living remnant of a time already legendary, and how many come because of something more than that, I do not know.

When some arrive, I see the disappointment in their faces on beholding, not an angel, but an old man enfeebled by passing time. Some arrive and would have me talk as though they are collecting an experience: they are meeting with John, and they want to tell others of this. Some arrive and wish to hear of Christ, of his apostles, of Mother Mary, Mary Magdalene, and the beginnings of our work—yet what they want is information, not resurrection. Some are interested, yet critical. Because each generation thinks itself more gifted with intelligence than the one that went before it, they consider me a simpleton in matters of the Spirit, and feel they would have served Our Lord with more effectiveness had they been his disciples—and perhaps they would have done, but still: their speculations are beside the point, for it was not their lot to be with him in person. Some go further still and see me as a heretic: they come here to argue or to stare. And some arrive, just two or three, who say a little awkwardly, 'Please teach me whatever you know, that I too may learn.'

One and all, I give them to drink of the water from my well, which is sweet and refreshing; and to them, one and all, I offer this remembrance of Lord Jesus and the knowledge he imparted that was later hidden or suppressed, the learning Thomas brought from India, and the secret of the Comforter to come.

THE REASONERS

And so, I want to speak of Christ—but how? There has first to be some knowledge of the Spirit, or whatever is said will be nothing but rumour and speculation.

For anyone can speak of Christ, and many do: but with what authority?

Consider, first, the reasoners—the ones who say that there is only relativity and who, accordingly, reject the Absolute. 'This talk of "the Spirit" may be pleasing to children, but we are more learned than that,' they maintain, 'and as for this business of resurrection, it is merely a fable, a dream. If your Jesus existed,' they go on, 'which, frankly, we doubt, then he was born in the typical way, not miraculously, and when he died on the cross, that was, of course, the end of him. All the rest is a myth.'

How weighty sound their statements! Yet turn them sideways and they are thinner than a leaf, being made of nothing more than thoughts—for thoughts have neither weight nor gravity.

While as for Christ: he was, and is, and always will be that which dwells beyond the reach of thought. And so, not all the thinking of these reasoners, not all their convoluted arguments, not all their pitting concept against concept, not all their serpentine philosophies can so much as touch his shadow.

Knowing nothing of divinity, these reasoners suppose divinity is nothing; knowing nothing of the truth, they think that truth is fantasy—when in reality the fault is not in truth or in divinity but in their feeling that through reason, with its insubstantial concepts, they can know all things and sit in judgement on them.

Why, though, should they want to catch the one who bodied forth pure wisdom in their nets of rationality? Why think the unsurpassable can be surpassed?

And why is it that they say, so proudly, 'We are our small selves only, there is nothing else'? Why not say, 'Mother and Father, we have need of your love'?

And why is it that they try to kill the sensitivity to God in others? Why not wish to have that sensitivity themselves?

And given that they have the concept of the Absolute, why is it that they do not search for its reality?

Why is it that they do not understand, through their intelligence, that that intelligence is limited? Why not admit that that intelligence is something they have found within themselves—whatever they have made of it, they did not first create it?

Why shut and lock the golden door through which they need to pass in order to envision Jesus as he is, the all-encompassing?

Instead, why not declare in all humility: 'We place our thinking at your feet, Lord God! We surrender our intelligence to you. Please give us truth instead!'

With their reason, it is true, they may tell us of the *how* of things—but it is not within their power to know the *why*, for their knowing lacks wisdom and love, it is empty of spirituality. Whether they should say, therefore: 'Yes, Jesus was a good man, we agree, but he was just a man and nothing more than that,' or whether they should say, 'This Christ was an impostor, he made unfounded claims about himself,' their opinions are entirely worthless, since they manifest no *gnosis*.

In short, these reasoners have not yet reached a point within themselves from which it is befitting that they speak of Christ.

But then, we brought our useless theories to him too. Time and time again we brought him valueless opinions as to what 'the Saviour' meant—and what was truth, and God, and Good, and Love, and how to live—and time and time again he had to say to us, 'Not this, not this, not that. You are searching in the Book of the Mind for that which is found in the Heart.'

I repeat this to these reasoners, yet they only laugh. 'Come, we will teach you how to reason, then you will see: the only truth is that there is no truth.'

One might as well argue with jackals and crows.

THE BELIEVERS

Yet what of the believers? When I hear our priests speak of our Lord so brazenly or casually, I find myself dismayed. They preach and practice rituals in his name, express their anger in his name and even frighten others in his name, but from where does the assurance come with which they do these things?

They say it is from their *belief*. But I ask: what is belief without truth? What value can conviction have, if not established first on knowledge—where by knowledge is meant *gnosis*? What use is all their preaching, bearing witness and baptising, without their having first become the Spirit? What use is their belief without its being *faith*, which is the knowledge of the heart? What use are words, and more words still, without there being *gnosis*?

Their mistake is in supposing that their passing feelings are substantial. They think those phantoms are more real than truth itself.

Moreover, they imagine that by saying they 'belong to Christ', it makes Christ belong to them—which is not so. The Divine may be invoked, but not confined. It may be offered invitations—with sincerity, decorously—but it can never be controlled, or organised, or owned. 'They will say, "We constructed a Church to contain you,"' said our Lord. 'And I shall answer,

"No, I was never there, that was a shadow you laid claim to, a shadow you imprisoned in your rites and texts and laws and definitions—a shadow, nothing more."'

He was so much more than the conceptions that we have of him. In the first place, he was not a conception, he was life itself. Nor was he simply here for human beings, his work had to do with the growth of the whole of Creation.

If I could, I would show him to you as he was, and you would be amazed.

When he had risen from the dead and I was with him once again, I understood that whatsoever I could see of him was but a fraction of some greater thing so vast that it contained that little room where he appeared to us, the city all around us with its streets and buildings and inhabitants, and, indeed, the world in its entirety and, up above, the starry firmament. It contained us all, just as—of course—it comprehends the one who writes this now. So, we should not attempt to crucify him once again with our beliefs and falsifying images and dead ideas.

Instead of bringing our beliefs and thoughts to him, like foolish maidens bearing vessels full of sand and pebbles to the well, we should empty out our minds of those impediments in order that his holiness might then be poured into the vessels of our hearts.

And when we speak of Christ, we should do so only from a knowledge of the Spirit, I believe—yet at times it eludes me as well, and then the children on the seashore with the ocean in their eyes seem far more learned, wise, and authorised to speak of truth than I.

THE CHILD KING

Even as a child I was seeking something. I would wander the hills in their colours of olive and ochre and think of the God who had made both those hills and their colours, and the sky and clouds and stars.

I loved the psalms of David and the book about Job, where God speaks out of the whirlwind, but most of all I loved the statements of Isaiah, when he spoke of the Lord to come. A child, I felt attracted to this boy-king who would sit on David's throne and rule the world with playfulness and love.

Yet the priests spoke sparingly of love and much about God's wrath. To them, I think that God himself was like an arch-priest whose approval could be won by knowledge of the scriptures, an observation of the rituals and a show of piety; or else he was a kind of usurer, who had lent us our lives at so costly a rate of interest that we were forever indebted to him, and who accepted no coin but that of ostentatious moral rectitude. When I saw how our priests behaved, I thought they had made burnt offerings of their lives.

They drew a picture of a God obsessed with Man's observance of the law in all its niceties—as though he had no eyes for other things, the things on which the law does not directly touch: the nobility of love, the beauty of the world. Not that I felt that God was careless of the law—yet I could not see him as a hard and ruthless judge, watching over men and women daylong and nightlong, yearlong and lifelong, keeping records of their sins. I thought: a father is firm with his children for their sake, but he does not have them spied upon nor does he condemn their mistakes outright, for if they cannot make mistakes, how are they to learn? If they are given no freedom, how can they grow?

And if a human father is like this, if he is forbearing and patient—then what of Almighty God?

God is innocent; not pedantic, suspicious or harsh, but innocent. And Jesus, too, was innocent. He was innocent of wanting things. He was innocent of desires except the one desire to carry out the task which brought him to this world. He was innocent of matter; no things of this Earth could cling to him. He was innocent of sin; no sins of any kind could be found in him. He was auspiciousness itself. He was spontaneity incarnate. He was the wisest of the wise. It is said by those who know that, in this world, he was the only incarnation of the archetype called *Shri Ganesha*.

And when he came to this world, it was not to impose the past upon us in the form of more conditioning, for he was innocent. Nor did he place us in thrall to the future, to be deluded by the small self's plans and dreams and expectations, for he was innocent. Nor did he know hatred, lust or greed. Nor was his wisdom overcast by preconceptions. Nor could he be befooled, or bought, or influenced by flattery, for he was innocent and saw all things with clarity: he saw things as they are.

As children do, he lived entirely in the present; as children are, he was forgiving; and as children can, he loved with simple spontaneity—for he was innocence embodied, he was the ageless child-king.

THE LAW

Intrinsic to us is a law—and if we transgress it, it reacts upon us: on our bodies, our feelings, our thoughts, our fate, our lives. If we wish to maintain our good health, we must observe this law; and if we wish to come into our birthright—that is, to enter the Kingdom of Heaven—we must first observe this law.

How do we know of this law? Through instinct and intuition, through practice and logic, through observations of Nature and the teachings of Moses.

This law is within us. It is that which sustains us. It is that which nourishes our growth as human beings. Its statutes are the ten commandments, it is the way of righteousness, and it leads to the Kingdom of God.

If we wander from it, we wander from that which sustains us. If we depart too far from it, we leave behind the narrow, true, ascending way. And therefore the prophets have sought to keep us to this lawful road: some through their visions and warnings, some by their calls to arms, some by founding laws enforced by punishments, and all by their example. But whatever the outward form they gave to it, the true law is within.

Moreover, this inner law is timeless and unchanging, whereas its outward form is relative. This latter form will vary here and there: from place to place, from time to time.

Yet to the Pharisees, the true law was the outward, manmade form, and they had further redefined and added to that form until it only served to limit and enslave us. They turned the Sabbath from a day of rest into a day of bondage, and through their notion that events had each their due, ordained response, they sought to banish from our lives all childlike vivacity and spontaneity, because they feared those qualities, they feared the marks of Nature blazoned forth in them, they feared the simple truth in them. Worse still, they gave us to believe that, in doing what they did, they represented God.

All my young life I resisted this. In my heart I thought that God Almighty was a God of love and innocence, that he must be kind and fatherly, compassionate and motherly. Yet I held to this thought with misgivings, for the Pharisees' word was law and that law was all around me, was in the air I breathed.

And so, it was with a sense of vindication and deliverance that I saw Jesus sever at a stroke the cords and knots which they had used to bind our souls, asserting with the confidence of absolute authority, 'The Sabbath was made for Man, not Man for the Sabbath.'

This was in the fields outside Capernaum, one day when the wheat was high.

JOHN THE BAPTIST

My first master was John the Baptist.

He was a man who had conquered the world. Hardship, thirst and hunger had no grip on him. He treated his body as a man treats a beast of burden; he ate locusts and wore the skins of wild animals. He was fierce and his passion for truth was fierce.

I was afraid of him.

But John was very great. Alone of us, apart from Mother Mary, he knew who Jesus was; and our Lord himself declared that no man more exceptional than John had yet been born. Though once, when I asked our Lord what need there had been for him to be baptised by John, Jesus answered quietly, not quite with a smile but with a look of thoughtfulness, as a king might think of a servant who had served him well and then died young, 'There was no need. It was simply done to please him.'

Then I felt as I feel now: that we are as children who play a game the name and form of which we have forgotten.

THE CALL

The first time I saw Jesus, I was in our father's boat beached by the Sea of Galilee. It was evening, my brother James was with me, we had brought the day's catch home and had begun to mend our nets—when all of at once I heard a voice some way along the shoreline, and I looked and saw the Son of God.

Yet I did not know that at the time. How could I have known that? I knew the men he was with—that is, Simon and Andrew—but who this stranger was I did not know. Yet something in his bearing drew my eyes as he approached, and when he stopped beside our boat and, in a voice of unpremeditated power, said: 'Follow me,' neither James nor I had any doubts about obeying him. Discarding our nets, we left our father's boat and followed him.

Later, James said that he thought he saw a child calling out to us across the water, when we first set eyes on him, whereas I seemed to see an ancient man who stood beyond the sea of time. There was all the gravity of majesty about him, while equally he seemed at rest within himself, and he moved upon the beach's shingle lightly, like a dancer. He moved as though all other men lived in a kind of darkness, and he alone within the light of day. He moved as though the elements knew him and welcomed him, bowed down before him and wished but to make him comfortable.

He moved as though he could have walked on water, had he had a mind to.

But I did not fully see these things just then, as I worked on our nets and watched him; I only felt them in my heart. For I did not know who he was, not with my mind alone. How could I have known who he was? And yet inside myself something did know who he was. Inside myself a recognition happened. Inside myself I saw with other eyes a man made all of light, so bright that one could scarcely look at him, with a flower in one hand and a pair of scales in the other, and, around him, the aura of God in the colours of fire, and under his feet, the starry sky, and that flower was like the sun. I saw on either side of him archangels armed with flaming swords. I heard with other ears the seraphs shout 'Hosanna!' I saw, inside myself, his face alive with measureless compassion. And yet with eyes of flesh I saw a figure on the seashore, calling, and no more than that, while above his head the seagulls cried their usual cries in the commonplace evening air.

And I remember that I glanced back at the waters on which, alternating and fleeting, the waves of light and darkness were displacing one another endlessly, and it seemed to me that, from the ocean of illusion, this man was calling me home.

WHOLENESS

Time after time they have asked me, 'But what was Jesus like? What sort of man was the Messiah?'

But I have to add to this another question, and ask, 'With what can one compare the incomparable?' Or: 'How can one encompass God in words?' One cannot, of course; it is impossible.

And yet we have to say something, for we must relate our knowledge and articulate our love. But let it be on the understanding that words are only words: at times they can contain and not release; they may obscure and not reveal.

Indeed, I have seen how men have drawn, from the few plain words of the Gospels, conceptions of Jesus that miss the mark—not because in themselves they are false, but because they do not indicate his *wholeness*. Such men seize on a statement here or there and say 'Jesus was meek' or 'Jesus was self-denying', or 'Jesus told the rich young man to give his wealth to the poor: therefore he cared most for the poor', or 'Jesus said that the poor will always be with us: therefore the poor were not his concern'—it is the rich who say that—and so on. But Jesus was neither the one thing nor the other: he was whole. He was the All, the *Pleroma*, the *Alpha* and *Omega*, the totality; he was whole.

Unlike ourselves, he had no angularities, or sharp or broken edges to his being. Unlike ourselves, he had no quirks or peculiarities, and because of that, he was resistant to description. For when we wish to describe one another, it is to our foibles and habits that we turn, just as we describe a man's face by its irregularities, by a birthmark or a scar. Jesus, though, was without any eccentricity. He was not divided in himself or more developed here and less so there. He was at one with himself, as well as with the sea's unerring tides and the movement of the stars.

He was whole. To the world's four directions he turned and blessed the seekers; he touched the four points of the compass in himself. He laughed at the antics of children and the nonsense of men engrossed in fleeting things with such portentousness, and at the priests with all their airs and graces, and always his laughter was like the sun: enlightening and brightening and warm.

He laughed, and he cried: I recall how he cried when the news was brought that Lazarus was dead. And how tears of compassion would start in his eyes if, say, a shepherd boy played on his pipe the lovely hill-country tunes for him; or if a stranger in a crowd were to listen with rapt intensity to his words, and then, instead of beseeching him for cures or charms, were simply to stand and bow as our Master passed; or if, among the eucalyptus trees of Capernaum, the townsfolk were to sing and dance their welcome to the Son of God—or if in other ways the glory and the beauty of humanity were expressed.

He cried and he laughed; he censured the hypocrites, the Pharisees, the Scribes, the lukewarm-hearted, and the merchants who, in their profiteering, cared so little for their fellow men or for the truth. He spurned the evil and cast out the *archons*, the demons, the ghosts. He was fiery, he was mild, he was tender to his brothers and his sisters, to his mother. He was playful, like a child. He was dignified, like a child. He was dynamic. He was whole. He was wholeness itself.

He knew the moods of men, but while we lived in those moods, one at a time, as though each mood were a dwelling-place, a cell, and we were inside them, he moved freely in and out of them, going where he chose.

For he was free. He was freedom in the form of the body. He knew the moods of men and women not as we know them, being lost in them, but freely, through his Spirit.

He was very different to others. I do not say that everyone recognised this, for many passed him by in the street without a second glance or waited on him at table with no awareness of his holiness, or even heard him preach without perceiving that this was someone unlike other men, someone transcendent and complete. Indeed, there were many who came to hear him, thinking only to test and judge him; and equally there were many who came to look at him, believing that if he were the Messiah, as rumour held him to be, they would know it at once—and always they went away saying, 'We are disappointed: this is but another man, like ourselves'—since that was what they wanted. They wished to be disappointed, in order that their own small selves might not be questioned and revealed. Moreover, they wished it to be known that they were fit to sit in arbitration over matters of the Spirit, when they knew nothing of truth, divinity, or Christ.

He was very different to others. But it is not true to say, as some have believed—ascribing such statements to me—that his form was magical, so that he was never seen to blink or close his eyes, for instance—though he did not move his eyes here and there haphazardly, as other men do—or that his feet left no prints in the sand, and so forth. Yet it is true that he sometimes seemed much taller than he really was, and sometimes seemed far stronger than a man of his stature could be, and that his person was miraculous, and that he sometimes appeared composed not of flesh but of light—so that once when the Pharisees tried to seize him, he simply disappeared. But no one saw him disappear; no one could prove these things; nor were they done to impress, or merely for effect.

He was altogether different from other men, yet he contained that difference that he might live among us as a friend. He broke his bread with us as though he were our father or our brother, and yet the whirlwind was at his command and the sea would have parted before him, had he asked it to. He broke bread with us and walked on the same earth as us and slept beneath the same stars as us, and yet he was the essence and the meaning of creation.

In the years when we knew him he was in the prime of life and the full bloom of health. He was tall and sturdy and had clay-coloured skin and dark, reddish hair, as though the blood of the Celts was in his ancestry. His face was strong and glowing, and his eyes shone with a kindness I have seen in no other face.

Never a word that he spoke was excessive, never a movement was wasted. When he moved, he was full of energy, and when he spoke, his words had power. They took effect. It is commonplace for rabbis and teachers to say: 'Truth is love' or 'Peace be with you' and the like, and indeed, any devil can say these things—and many have, and many will—but only the truly holy man invests them with auspiciousness and grace. Should a devil say, 'Peace be with you,' nothing comes of it but, in the end, self-delusion and strife; but when Jesus said these words, then angels bearing gifts of sweet contentment came discreetly to those receptive to his love.

As for his worldly life, he was skilled in his father's trade, that of carpentry. Indeed, he was a master-craftsman, and in Palestine today one still meets with men who will say with pride, 'I have a table' (or a chair or a yoke or some such object) 'made by Jesus of Nazareth.' Also, at some time in his youth he had served as a carpenter on one of his great-uncle's trading ships and had journeyed to Britannia, where lead and tin are mined.

And there are many tales of his childhood: some fictitious and some true. But for his part, Jesus did not speak of the past, preferring to live in the present. And there was something in his mood that focused our attention on the here and now, so that while we wondered as to what his childhood had been, we did not question him about it, nor did he encourage us to do so. If men talked about their past, he would say, 'But now the past is over, is a dream, no longer real,' while to those who praised him as the one whom the prophets had promised, he would reply: 'Yes, that is so. Now let us leave behind the promise and live with its fulfilment.'

I know that he had not undertaken any special course of study, as some men claim. He had not lived among the Essenes, as has been rumoured; nor had he toiled in the schools of Egypt. On the contrary, he would say of the Egyptians that, although they knew much about death, they knew little of God. No: as to where he got his knowledge from, it was simply that he was the *Logos*. He was the *Alpha*. He knew everything from the beginning.

And such, then, was the transcendent omnipotent God, the Pantocrater, who shared his bread and his life with us among the high, parched hills of Judea and by the shores of the Sea of Galilee, all those years ago . . .

HIS BIRTH

It was in the waning of the year when Mary and her husband Joseph came to Bethlehem, brought by the census ordered by Augustus Caesar. But the village's inn being full, they were forced to shelter in the stable for the night.

And there the animals themselves bowed down in front of Mary and gave her of their warmth against the bitter winter cold.

And no moon shone in the sky above Judea that night, for, according to the men of India, it was the darkest night of all the year: the night on which they light the lamps in all the rooms of all their houses, it being their Festival of Lights or, as they say, *Diwali*.

And on that darkest of dark nights, at midnight, Lord Jesus Christ was born. It was then that he had to be born because he was the Light, and the Light had to come into the darkness of the world. For the world was possessed by ghosts and shadows, and by the darkness of our ignorance of God, and by the gloom of superstition and conditioning, and by the dense opacity of Man's small self, and by the black obscurity of human cruelty; and into that deep darkness he who was the light within his mother's eyes when she looked upon the sufferings of men and women who were lost, not knowing where to turn for comfort, he who was the light of God's compassion streaming forth into the midnight of the world, he who was the Light incarnate—had to come.

THE STABLE

Yet because he was the Lord of Lords, he might have said: 'I shall take my birth in Herod's house,' or 'I shall be born in Rome, as Caesar's heir, that everyone may know me as their Lord.'

But no, he took his birth in Bethlehem, in the quiet hill-country of Judea.

Or again, he might have said, 'I shall see that I am born in comfort, in a rich man's mansion.' At the very least, he might have said: 'Let me be born within the four stone walls of Joseph's house.'

But no, he came into this world inside a stable where, as a rule, not even the poorest of the poor are born.

For truth is unconcerned with wealth, or power, or whatever the comfort that matter might offer.

Moreover, as a bride is veiled, so truth prefers to mask itself a little from the undeserving. Or perhaps it is not that truth is masked, but that the undeserving—who, on this side, are the arrogant, and on that, the frivolous, subservient and parasitical—are blind to truth when it is right in front of them, because their vision is distorted by their small self and conditioning.

Besides, the truth prefers the company of innocence and wisdom: of shepherds, and magi, and the beasts of the field: to that of slavish or worldly men.

THE CENSUS

The life that Jesus lived was a symbolic one. What he did and what was done to him: these things were resonant with meaning.

So: he was born during Caesar's enrolment—and what Caesar Augustus performed in the gross, when he called home his people to be gathered and numbered, our Lord came to do in the subtle.

He summoned from the fields, the seas and the mountains the prodigal, questing souls; he called from their burdensome lives the errant and sorrowing ones; he cried out: 'Come home! Come home!' to every lost seeker of meaning; he beckoned the lovers of truth to the gates of the City of God. More, he said in effect to all human beings: it is time to take stock of yourselves, to know where you have come from and where you are going.

For he on whose head they placed a crown of thorns was in reality the ruler of the world—the ruler, and its judge.

THE WISE MEN

Presaging something marvellous, a bright new star shone in the sky when Christ was born—and guided by it light, three wise men made their way to Bethlehem, there to find him in the manger and adore him.

Now, these three men were *magi* from the land of Persia or beyond. But they were also more than that: they were nothing less than the *Trimurtis*, the three great forms of God described in India as *Brahma*, who creates, as *Vishnu*, who sustains, and as *Shiva*, who bestows existence and its opposite, destruction. And, in worshipping Christ, they were praising the essence of things, the quintessence of holy wisdom, the pure power of God as a child.

It was from Thomas, my brother disciple, who afterwards went to India, that I learned of this.

THE STAR

As for the star itself, some say it was in fact two planets in conjunction: the one being Saturn, representing Christ's Father, and the other one Jupiter, representing his Mother—as though both of his heavenly parents were gazing with love upon Bethlehem, when Jesus Christ was born.

THE GESTURE

Often, in later years, Lord Jesus would lift his right hand in blessing, with the thumb, the third and little fingers folded over, but the first and second fingers raised. I saw him do this many times, yet failed to wonder what it meant, beyond the fact that it was a *mudra* of authority. But now I know that these two fingers meant for him, respectively, Lord Krishna and Lord Vishnu: God the Father incarnate, and God the preserver, of which he was himself the greater form, *Shri Mahavishnu*. In other words, they represented two aspects of his Father, so that when he raised his hand like that, he was saying in effect, 'I am doing my Father's business. As I wish, therefore, let it be so.' This was explained to me long afterwards, by Mary in Jerusalem.

HIS NAME

Yeshoda, Krishna; Jesus Christ. To those who listen, there are echoes in Christ's name of Krishna, the great dark lord of India—who, as I say, was God in the form of the Father, Jehovah. And in the name of Jesus, one can also hear the name Yeshoda, who fostered Krishna as a child.

For Jesus was the *Alpha*, the first of the letters inscribed in the Book of Creation. And thus his profound, majestic personality was not invented at his birth in Bethlehem: it existed before, and long before. He is not the master of our age alone, but the prince of all eternity.

Sometimes those clever ones, the questioners, say, 'Jesus, yes, "the resurrected god"—we have heard that myth before. You Christians have copied the dreamers of Egypt, with their fantastic tale of Osiris.' But what Jesus did amongst us here on Earth he practised first in the eternal world. Perhaps, then, those myths are intimations of that first venture in the world beyond the world.

And because he is eternal, it is not surprising that a thousand years or more ago the Druids knew him as their *wondrous youth*. Or that he was entitled *Mahavishnu* in the Indian *Puranas*. Or that the prophets foretold him. Or that John the Baptist was his herald.

Nor is it so surprising that he should have had, just like an artist's name upon a work of art, the name of God the Father inscribed within his own name, *Jesus Christ*.

PLAY

The story goes that once, when Jesus was a child, he was playing on the road beside a dirty stream of running water. First, he made the stream into three channels, and where those channels met was where the rubbish, leaves and pebbles in the stream had gathered, blocking it. Then, with a single word, he made the dirty water in those channels clean, and with a single gesture swept the dam of filth and stones aside, so that the water poured into the pool beyond. And his mother, who was standing there beside him, smiled, for she understood that this diversion with the water in the gross world was an image of the work he had to do inside the subtle world within, and that although he was a little boy no more than five years old, still he was like a craftsman planning out the task before him. And then she frowned because she knew that only through a crucifixion could he sweep that dam aside in human beings.

But our Lord consoled her, saying not to worry, for both this game with water at the roadside and the work he had yet to perform in the subtle, invisible channels within were play and play alone.

And those channels were the *Nadis* in our being, stated Thomas, while the dam stood for the *Adi Agnya Chakra* at the gate of the pool of life—or as it is otherwise called, the beautiful Kingdom of Heaven.

PERFECTION

Jesus was perfect.

I have heard men assert—out of envy, perhaps, or with a certain cleverness—that in spite of all his qualities he was not yet perfect, for one day near Jerusalem—here they reach for an instance—he cursed a fig tree to wither and die.

But this was not done out of petulance or weakness, as those who want to judge Christ think. It was done as a sign. It was done out of wisdom. For the tree in question bore no fruit, and in condemning it our Lord made plain the fate of those whose lives are fruitless, who disregard the Spirit. Today, they are dead within, for nothing living comes from them; but tomorrow, if they do not seek their Spirit, they may find themselves on the outside of the circle of existence.

Then, there are agnostics who suppose our Lord was moved to doubt himself when on the cross. Had they been on Golgotha, however, they would have seen him surrender his body, not in despair, but like a king in battle. They would have seen him play the part it was his choice to play until the very end, while inwardly unmoved. And they would have said, just like the Centurion who stood beneath him, guarding him, 'Indeed, indeed, this was the Son of God!'

Now, others think he was a saint or prophet, yes, that much they will allow—but nothing more than that. And they add that it was Paul who later reinvented him, calling Jesus the 'Messiah'. But while Jesus was not in the least ambitious, not in the way that Paul, say, was ambitious, still as the sun shines forth without apology, with neither pride nor diffidence, so his divinity shone forth and could be felt by those who were receptive, for in truth he was the Son of God.

And so, he was divine - and because he was divine, whatever he did was auspicious. It is true that there seemed nothing preconceived about his comments or his deeds. It is true that they seemed no more thought out in advance than if, for instance, he were to have picked up a handful of cubes of mosaic and strewn them on the ground. Yet if one had then looked down, one would have seen that automatically, spontaneously, those *tesserae* had formed a pattern. For he was perfect, and naturally, spontaneously, whatever he did had coherence, shape and meaning. Still more, it had *benevolence*.

It was not that he thought, 'I shall do such and such, and it will ever after be a symbol for humanity.' Instead, he acted in accordance with his nature, and because he was divine, whatever he did was symbolic. Nor do I believe that he fulfilled the sayings of the prophets by design. Rather, because he *was* divine, his actions could not help but bear their sayings out.

He was perfect, and therefore beyond temptation. I remember once, one harvest time, I began to wonder at the nature of his miracles—imagining, naively, the mechanics of divinity to be a sort of conjuring—and inside myself I questioned what he did when he was not with us but on his own in prayer; and thus I took to watching him, as though to catch him unawares. But one day he grabbed my beard and pulled me sharply towards him, saying firmly: 'John, do not doubt me, nor be inquisitive.' Ashamed, I made-believe I did not understand him, at which he frowned and turned away. But the harvest moon waxed and waned again, and the place where he had tugged my beard still hurt. Then, being more at ease by now, I said: 'Oh Master, if your playful tug has caused such pain, what would it be like if you had hit me?' Far from smiling, though, he answered indirectly, saying: 'John, from now on do not try to tempt the one who cannot be tempted.'

Yet this was a minor matter. It is said that when he went into the wilderness to consider the task before him and how it might be best accomplished, the whole Creation's negativity personified came forth to tempt him, and it was utterly confounded.

For Jesus was perfect. He was the perfect man, the immaculate one, the virgin-born, the Son of God.

WINE

Still others say that Jesus was divine—that, yes, he was the Son of God—yet, all the same, like ordinary human beings he frequently drank wine. And once at a wedding in Cana, they add, he even made it out of water.

When they make this claim, they are reacting, perhaps, to those who would depict our Lord as moralistic and austere. Or, feeling rebellious, they want that he should also have rebelled. Beyond these things, however, what they really want is Christ's approval of *their* drinking. They would like it that, in his behaviour, he sanctioned their affection for intoxicants.

But they are wrong.

Christ's awareness was pure; he would never have wished to pollute it with wine. Christ's being was holy; he would never have wished to insult it with alcohol. Christ's attention was subtle; he would never have wished to confuse it or blunt it with gross, fermented drink.

Or is it that they think that Jesus, who personified spontaneity, was so disabled with inhibitions that he needed wine to numb his fear, unblock his tongue? Do they think that the one who incarnated joy had need of wine to make him happy?

He looked with compassion on those who, for this reason or that, were corrupting their being—but he never believed that, to cure them, he first had to poison himself.

As for the water he transmuted into wine in Cana—its taste was of sweet, unfermented grape juice, and that is all.

THE LION

A man could not have done what Jesus did, nor have spoken as he spoke, nor have loved as he loved, had he not been absolutely without fear.

Consider how the Scribes and Pharisees opposed him. Even when, as a boy of twelve years old, he talked with them inside the Temple in Jerusalem, his wisdom's subtle probing far outstripped their sluggish, laboured reasoning in matters of the Spirit, and when he preached his gospel as a grown man, they saw him as a danger to their way of life—for they were growing wealthy with their profits from the Temple market and their share of the people's offerings, and they feared he might stir up the masses against them. So, day after day they questioned him, threatened him, mocked him - yet in vain, for he was not disturbed.

His existence was an affront to their behaviour, therefore they wanted his life. He knew this; he had taken their measure; he went his own way regardless.

When they brought the woman taken in adultery and asked if they should stone her as Mosaic law required, he simply stooped down and wrote on the ground as though he had not heard them. Again, and with avidity, and with cunning masked as righteousness, they demanded a response. They thought they had outwitted him at last, since he would either have to say the law was wrong, or else would have to punish her himself. I was there, I saw them, and though they had the form of men, they seemed as vicious and ravening wolves around a lamb that had strayed from the flock, while Jesus was the shepherd whom they thought would have to flee or be himself devoured.

Yet he was neither frightened nor confused. Unhurriedly he raised his head and with a few words sent them packing. And then and there the woman, Mary Magdalene, perceived him as divine.

Now, because Isaiah had called the future Lord *a man of sorrows*, some believe he was a thin, frail, under-nourished man. He was not. He was strongly-built—for, after all, he was a carpenter and not an invalid—and whenever one was near him, one had the feeling one was near the source of life itself.

Again, because he was born in a stable and blessed the meek and suffered himself to be crucified, there are men of our faith who believe he was a humble, soft-spoken, retiring man. Yet how can the Divine be retiring and meek when it knows itself to be divine? How can a man be humble when he knows he is the Lord of Lords, the King of Kings? And how could a reticent, diffident man have preached his gospel in the very teeth of those who hated him? Or have denounced the scribes and priests as hypocrites and thieves? Or have described them even to their faces as the sons of hell?

If in his actions he was humble, it was for our sake, that we might imbibe humility. Or it was so that men might not attack him for behaving like a king, or for being outspoken—since to have done so would have been their undoing.

But timidity and slavishness were foreign to his nature. Nor could he ever compromise with sin. And when he cleansed the Temple in Jerusalem, before the Passover, not a speck of fear was found on him. Into that throng of businessmen and usurers, of stallholders haggling over prices, of inspectors vetting animals for sacrifice, of priests accepting offerings for sin and thanks and trespass, of moneychangers selling sanctuary coin, he advanced with a whip in his hand—and not one of them thought to withstand him. We followed in his wake as he overturned their tables and spilled their goods and money on the floor and drove out their sheep and oxen and loosed their doves into the air, proclaiming in a voice that resounded from floor to roof and wall to wall, 'You have made of my Father's house a den of thieves!' And we trembled as much at his own overpowering energy as at their numbers and the order of things they represented; while the poor and the seekers applauded, for they saw that here, at last, was their champion.

Men say he was the Lamb of God, and so he was. But in him the lion lay down with the lamb, and he was the Lion of God as well.

MARY MAGDALENE

I remember Mary Magdalene, the day she first came to Lord Jesus. As a brother would welcome a sister who might have erred, but who was nonetheless the sister of his heart, so he welcomed her then.

We could not understand how one so pure could countenance one so impure.

But then we saw that just because he was so pure, he knew that no error could touch him, no sin could be ascribed to him.

And then we saw that we ourselves in other ways were still less pure than Mary Magdalene, and we felt ashamed.

Yet he only laughed at our shame, or, rather, he laughed with us at our shame, so that we should see that guilt is as impure as that which it is based upon.

For in truth we are not these impurities, we are the Spirit.

HER DEFERENCE

At first Mary Magdalene would hold herself aloof from us—and I was pleased at this, believing that her deference towards us, who were the first disciples, was only right and proper. Also, she never pressed herself upon Lord Jesus, although she was waiting and willing to serve him at all times. This too I found pleasing, because it would not have seemed correct that an adulteress should be at ease with Christ and Christ's disciples.

Then I saw that this deference was far from being based on an awareness of her former state. Indeed, to all intents and purposes she had forgotten what she had been, had forgotten the past and had no thought of the future, but was living instead in the present, which is the presence of God, and if she deferred to Lord Jesus, it was because she saw precisely who he was.

We too knew who he was, but where we saw the lark or the eagle, she saw the phoenix in its glory.

And the reason why she kept herself apart from us was not because she was ashamed but because she could not comprehend how we could be so familiar with the Son of God.

THE SISTER

Our Lord and Mary Magdalene were as brother and sister: though born of different families, that was their relationship, and they epitomised the pure connectedness of that relationship.

One day in the height of summer, in a garden in Bethsaida—one day when Mary Magdalene was absent—Lord Jesus said to us: 'As I am with Mary, so I would wish you to be with every woman who is not your wife or in another way your relative. They are your sisters, you are their brothers, and that bond is one of innocence.'

If it seemed that, in saying these words, he was setting a limit upon us, then know that, as a house has its walls or a body its skin, our behaviour has its borders. Such limits are there to sustain us; they give us balance and security.

And when we live within these limits, we feel no constraint, for when we live within the law, the law must leave us free.

So, let it be with our attention as with the water in that garden where he spoke those words. Had it been spread here and there indiscriminately, it would have quickly dried up, and the lilies and grass would have withered. And then the Spirit, who is the enjoyer, would have come there no more, for what would there have been to enjoy?

But when our attention is channelled between proper limits, as the water was there, then the garden of our being will be nourished and our character have depth.

And as for those who think that secretly, within himself, he may have wished to marry Mary Magdalene, thus exchanging his life of the Spirit for the life of a commonplace man—how little they know of that Spirit! How little they know about God!

And as for those who think that, for her part, Mary may have wished to be the bride of Christ—how little they know of that love in which nothing is needed, no object is craved—for whoever can love in that way is already fulfilled.

And if they should say, as sometimes they say, 'Oh, but that story made Christ seem more human,' I would answer: 'Of what use is that? For if by "more human" you mean "more like you, with your defects, desires and confusion," then how could our Lord be the Way and the Light and the Spirit incarnate?'

MARRIAGE

Of marriage itself, he said, on that afternoon in the garden: 'I am not here to marry, but I do not say that you should not take wives or husbands, for the way that leads towards the kingdom is the way of balance. Yet if by chance or out of choice you go unmarried, do not do so in my name.'

As for men who are drawn towards men, and women who are drawn towards women, here Jesus said mysteriously, not scornfully but with concern, that same afternoon in the garden, 'Would they have the sun shine day and night? Or the stars shine night and day?'

POETRY

Even had I not known Jesus, nor learned about his miracles, nor seen his resurrected self, I think the beauty of the words he spoke would yet have told me: 'This is the Son of God'.

Not that he wrote any books, or wished to write books. His tablet was the human heart: his instrument, his voice.

And everything he spoke was a poem in praise of humanity, was a poem of thanksgiving to God.

I say 'in praise of humanity' since he cared for Man. It was because he cared for Man and knew what he was capable of that he did not spare him or talk down to him. Besides which, he put on the body of Man and named himself the Son of Man, he ate Man's food, he used Man's speech.

And all his words were poetry. When he preached in the Temple it was poetry, or when he said as we set out at dawn, with a gesture towards the east: 'See the rising sun, how it clothes itself in red and gold, how it journeys forth across the sky untiringly, because it too loves Man,' that also was poetry. And then, glancing back at the place we had left, 'But Man does not love himself.

'If Man could see the beauty of these stones lying in the road he would rejoice; but if he saw the beauty of his brothers and his sisters in their Spirit he would weep and turn towards his Father saying, "I did not know! I could not conceive of such glory!"'

THE SUN

Men look up at the sun when it shines above Ephesus and are thankful for its light and warmth, knowing there would be no life without it. But they do not examine the sun, they do not peer at it through lenses in case their eyes are burned; nor do they bare their skin indiscreetly to its light. They treat it with respect.

And so it was with Jesus. For all his sweetness and warmth, he was such that none of us who knew him well would have taken liberties with him. Not that he once spoke unkindly to us, but there was that in his character: an inherent majesty: which precluded any mischievousness or insubordinate behaviour or excessive familiarity on the part of those around him.

Even Judas felt this, I believe, for until the end the sly and bitter demon in his nature was subdued in front of Christ.

Even the Pharisees were aware of this, I think, for in spite of their hostility, they did not dare to apprehend him by themselves. When they brought forth Mary Magdalene to test him, and he said: 'Let whoever is sinless among you throw the first stone at me,' they drew back and dispersed, scorched by the light of his truth. And often they would question and accuse him, and then—when he moved—part before him, though he was only one man, unarmed, and they were many.

And even Pilate felt this, when it was said that Jesus had named himself the Son of God. Fear gripped him as he looked at Christ, though our Lord was but a single man, a prisoner, and friendless among the Jews, while Pilate had armed guards around him, his favourites by his side, the Sanhedrin in attendance—and, in his person, the whole authority of Rome.

THE RESTING-PLACE

There were times when I think that Jesus knew a certain loneliness—for with whom could he share his divinity?

We were men and women, not gods. Our province was everyday life, its inhabitants our neighbours, its borders our conventions, its concerns the petty issues that engaged us from moment to moment . . . while his province was the world. It was the universe. His horizons were—where? Beyond the star-filled sky . . . while ours consisted of the hills about Lake Tiberias.

We could not comprehend his holiness.

Once in Capernaum in the early days of his ministry, we found ourselves surrounded by a host of men and women puzzled and intrigued in equal measure by our Master's teachings, or curious to see his face, or eager to be healed of some infirmity; all talking among themselves and shouting at him to look in their direction: one lady pleading in nonsensical broken words with him, another coughing and crying, another asking our Lord to explain, or justify, some point he had made in his discourse—I can hear that man's indefatigable, querulous voice even now—a fourth requesting something—a blessing, perhaps—and Jesus in the midst of them, being harried from street to street as we walked towards the harbour, yet displaying compassionate patience with this beckoning, jostling crowd, while at the same time, I felt, impatient for something that was lacking there: the desire to know Divinity, a pure and ardent wish to have the truth.

All at once, there was a pause. Then Jesus spoke, saying: 'Foxes have holes, and the birds of the air have their nests, but the Son of Man has nowhere to lay his head.' And as he said this he gazed at the crowd intently, as though he were looking at them from a long way off, or as though he were veiled from them, as much as by his human form as by the white dust which, in their enthusiasm, they had kicked up all around him.

Just so I see him looking at them, in my memory, with the sea behind him, a line of palms swaying slightly in the breeze, a boat tied up on the shore.

At first I wondered what our Saviour's meaning was, for it would not have been so difficult, among all these inquisitive people, to find him somewhere to stay for the night. But the resting-place he sought was not outside, out there, within Capernaum or in the wider world, but in our very selves. Yet how many amongst us were saying, 'Lord of Lords, please enter my awareness'?

At such times, he seemed the only true, substantial man amid a world of ghosts.

And later, when, in spite of his injunctions that we love each other, we would squabble over trivialities, he would look at us gravely, with impatient detachment—as though it were simpler by far for him to share his nature with the birds or the trees or the rocks beneath his feet than with those he had come to save.

THE STRANGER

There were times, as well, when he spoke as though his understanding were a burden to him, for what was plain to him seemed obscure to us, and try as he might, he could not impart what he wished to impart. It was as if he were a foreigner, and was describing in a tongue we did not know a place we could not imagine.

This was when he discoursed on the Kingdom of God.

Yet seeing how little we followed, he tried both with gestures and hints, in plain speech and riddles, in symbols and stories, in the exercise of logic and the play of poetry to express himself, to explain himself, that we might understand.

The road to that Kingdom within us, and the whereabouts of its borders, and how to find its narrow, guarded gate, and how to pass through that gate—all this he wished to tell us, to prepare us for the days to come.

And this was his mission on Earth: not to bind us to an old or new morality, not to institute moral laws, or a system of ethics; not to found a worldly power, a Church, a Christendom; not to dominate, or inculcate guilt and fear; but to stir our souls to seek our liberation, and to describe that liberation, and to nourish our lives, and, principally, to make that liberation possible. And to exemplify that liberation in himself. This above all was his mission and this is what he did.

He was not here to found an Earthly power but to open Earth to Heaven.

But although he said clearly: 'My Kingdom is not of this world,' still many looked to him to found an empire or establish a theocracy—and many still try to do this on his behalf.

And although he said: 'My Kingdom is within you,' still many conceived of a city of dreams outside this life, where only the dead would know truth.

And although he said: 'The Kingdom of Heaven is spread across the Earth, but you do not see it,' there are those who consider the world to be in essence evil.

And although he said: 'The Kingdom is present already, but you are not aware of it,' there are many who think he has yet to create it.

And although he said: 'The Kingdom of Heaven is among you,' and 'Love your brother like your soul, guard him like the apple of your eye,' still there are many who turn their backs on their fellows and seek the Kingdom in isolation.

And although he said: 'Unless you become like an innocent child, the Kingdom is closed to you,' still many behave as though by means of pomp and ritual, by assuming titles such as 'father' or 'archbishop', or through doing good works, or through hurting their bodies, or through fasting, or through indulging their every desire in the sacred name of truth, or through other forms of effort, thought or artifice, they will arrive in the Kingdom of God.

Again and again we misunderstood him, or misinterpreted him, or interpreted him to suit our fleeting desires and our own small self.

And that is why I say that although he was the Word, the *Logos*, the power of the Holy Spirit that informed the whole Creation, and although he befriended and loved us and even went so far as to wash the feet of his disciples, truly Jesus must have felt himself to be a stranger in this world.

THE BIRDS

It is said that once, when he was five years old, he made twelve sparrows out of clay. A passer-by, observing him fashion these toys, complained to his father Joseph that his son was working on the Sabbath. Joseph went and asked the boy what he was thinking of. In reply, the child clapped his hands and ordered: 'Go!'

And behold, the twelve clay birds took wing and flew away.

Much later, in Jerusalem, I asked our Lord if this were true. His answer was to gaze at us, his twelve disciples, as though to say, 'Birds of clay have no doubts, nor do they think they know the truth when truth is nowhere near them. But now I have to give reality to men who think they live already, not knowing they are toys of clay.'

THUNDER

One day when the weather was cold we came to a town in Samaria where, by way of a greeting, they gave us not flowers but suspicion, not interest but laughter. Some devotees of Mithras had been there before us—and not only them, but a fortune-teller from the north as well, a man who had turned the people's heads with his wild, extravagant talk. Thus, the elders had had enough of strangers interrupting the slow rhythm of their lives with tales of repentance and salvation, and they cold-shouldered us. To them, we were hawkers of dreams, not bringers of truth. To them we appeared as though spellbound. And what kind of person had worked this strange magic upon us? Neither hermit nor priest, nor some wise man from over the sea, but a carpenter's son from Nazareth.

Of those who came to hear him preach, some few stood at a distance, watchfully, as if he were there for their entertainment—while others cross-questioned him sharply, a heckler in the pay of the priests shouted out at him, and even those few seekers who did come forward appeared lukewarm and sceptical. They wished to see miracles, yes—but not the fundamental miracle of their own enlightenment.

Now, this was towards the end of his ministry, and time and time again our Lord had proved his spirituality, had established his divinity: indeed, he had epitomised the truth in every act and every word; yet still these people wished for signs and omens, for supernatural phenomena, and still they were suspicious of his motives—as if the work of their everyday lives were more important by far than the gift of eternity.

But worse was to come. At the gates of the neighbouring town, the authorities turned us away.

James and I were incensed by the sloth of these people, by their hostility and apathy, by their treatment of our Saviour and—in retrospect I see—not least by their treatment of us. And so that night we went to Jesus, saying, 'Shall we pray for fire from heaven to destroy these people utterly, as happened in Elijah's time?'

To our surprise, our Lord rebuked us firmly, saying: 'Do you think I have come to meet the righteous only? Have I come to address perfected men?

'If a man is pure he does not need my word: he has heard it already, has adhered to my way, is already washed clean.

'But for those who are striving for truth: for them I have come.

'For the little ones lost in the dark wood at the time of the rains: for them I have come.

'For the little ones lost in the ghost-haunted wood at the time of the storm: for them I have come.

'For the women who know the thorns of life, but not the flower: for them I have come.

'For the men who in their words and deeds have trampled on the flowers of life and then, when it is evening, cry out: "We did not know what we were doing!"—for them I have come.

'For Man, who wishes to harvest joy, but sows only pain and sorrow: for him I have come.

'For Man, whose inmost wish is for liberation, and yet who day and night revolves the wheel of desire with one hand, and night and day revolves the wheel of action with the other, and so must suffer; for him I have come.

'So, do not talk of judgement but of mercy. Rest assured, there will be a time for judgement, when Almighty God declares: "Just so much—and no more," but that time is not yet, and that judgement is not your concern. Your business is not to condemn but to save: first your own self, then others. Your business is to mediate the Holy Ghost's compassion: in all ways, in all forms, at all times.'

Then he smiled, and called us *Boanerges*, meaning 'Sons of the thunder'.

However, knowing that in our rage there was an element of purity, since we were angry at the disrespect which they had shown the Son of God—and an element of puzzlement, because we could not understand how men could ignore his wisdom, or drift away from his Gospel—nor could we understand why God did not move everyone to flock to him, strewing palm leaves before his feet and garlanding him with flowers; knowing all of this, he said:

'Within themselves, men are free to be slaves of their own small selves, or slaves of their conditioning, or slaves of them both if they wish, and the

Son of Man has come not to rob them of that freedom but to give them more freedom.'

And I understood him to mean that if they did not choose the freedom of the Spirit, not even God with all his powers and angels would override their will. Not that he could not override it if he chose, but that Man should have the freedom to accept his bondage or his liberation within himself: this belongs to the form of the world as the Holy Spirit has made it, and God will not willingly change it.

So, on hearing this I became thoughtful, and regarded the people of those towns not with antipathy, nor quite with sympathy, but with pity for their dull, insipid souls, their discontentment, and their fate.

GUILT

There was a time when in Jesus's presence I felt ashamed. When he spoke of the man who had buried the talent the rich man had lent him, I thought of myself. When he said that: 'Blessed are the pure in heart,' I saw my soul as indelibly stained with cupidity, anger and lust. When he spoke of 'the place of the gnashing of teeth', I imagined implacable wrathful angels escorting me there forthwith. In short, I saw humanity's sins within my own being, and when Jesus was near, I shrank from him. I was no longer the 'son of the thunder' that he had called me, but one weakened by fears that had no distinct shape or form.

Jesus said nothing.

We were travelling a great deal at this time, and every day, wherever we were, a crowd of people would leave their tools, their nets, their business, their housework, and come to hear Jesus talk; yet I felt like a stranger among them. On being made aware that I was one of Christ's apostles, some regarded me with veneration—but the more respect they showed me, the more I felt myself to be an actor whose imposture was about to be exposed. The least of them seemed rich in self-belief compared with me. I saw the hope in their eyes, heard the mirth in their talk as they made their way home from Christ's sermons, and I felt I had failed myself and God: for all around me there was happiness, yet I alone, it seemed, was ill at ease. I told myself to be calm; I told myself to have faith; I told myself to be glad—for surely we disciples were the favoured ones . . . and yet I was unhappy. And that in such a position I should feel no joy made my weight of guilt feel more cumbersome still—for it was guilt that I was feeling, guilt that had possessed me, guilt that had embraced me as its own.

Still Jesus said nothing.

In my dreams I saw the ascent as a long and precipitous climb. I saw my companions advancing to the mountain top with ease, but when it came to my turn to go forward, the pathway narrowed, the slope abruptly steepened, jagged rocks showered down around me; I could not move for fear of falling.

Then one day Christ took me aside and said: 'John, what are you afraid of?'

I did not know what to say. I thought: of nothing definite, of everything indefinite. I said: 'Of you, Lord.'

He did not reply by saying anything that I might have expected. Instead he said: 'There was a king who one day had dealings with three people. The first was the prince of another country, who was his enemy. This prince was brought into his presence and was astounded by his power. The second person was a petty criminal, a wrongdoer guilty of sin. He had to interview the man prior to judging him. And the third was the son who loved him.

'Now, two of those people were afraid of the king, but the third was not. Who was that third?'

I answered: 'His loving son,' and Jesus nodded.

'And why?'

Without pausing for thought I replied: 'Because he loved him.'

'You have said it. Because he loved him, and love cannot co-exist with fear.

'But do you think the son was perfect? Do you think his soul was unblemished? Still, he was his father's son and he knew it. He loved his father and it was with this love that he identified, not with his faults; thus, he was unafraid.

'So, open your heart to me and have no fear,' said the Lord of all the worlds, and waved his hand at the hills above Gennesaret, asleep in the evening light. 'No more than you would wish to think of the worms in the dirt when you look at this landscape before you do I wish to rest my eyes on the darkness now within you.

'So, open your heart and have no fear.

'It is true: I am the Light, and of its own accord this Light reveals the soul. But do not be afraid, for while it is a revelation it is also a dissolution, and the more that this Light is allowed in your heart, the more it disperses the darkness surrounding your Spirit.

'So, open your heart to me and have no fear. For the Son of Man is eager to enter the hearts of men, but it is not in his nature to enter them uninvited.'

WATER

Jesus did not react.

To watch him respond to foolish questions or demanding situations was to see a stone thrown into water. The water is untroubled, it neither rejects the stone nor is changed by it, but makes of its impact an image, a pattern. Just so did Jesus decorate himself with what had been intended as insulting or dismissive; just so did he make meaning out of nonsense, laughter out of anger, and beauty out of conflict.

Stone after stone the Pharisees rained down upon the living water of his being, yet never once did he react. He did not react to things outside himself; his actions were not conditioned. In encountering the world, his attention was not drawn in and overpowered, nor was it repelled. Neither could others disturb him, nor could they flatter him. Detached, clear-eyed, benevolent, he was the witness of whatever happened, and his actions sprang forth from his own pure, abounding compassion. They came not out of some exchange or give and take with the world, but from himself. Their foundation was his heart.

Yet in a way he did not even act, for his Father acted through him, or, as Jesus said, in everything he simply did his Father's bidding. Whenever he spoke or he moved, or decided a route to be followed or a thing to be done, he did so immediately, without taking thought and debating the matter within himself—without first creating a subject, an action, an object. While we say 'I do this' or 'I do that', with Jesus there was but a doing, or a being.

It was as though there flowed through him eternal life, and it was eternal life that was born and lived and died and upraised itself in triumph in the form of Jesus Christ of Nazareth.

THE DYER

Nothing pleased Jesus more than that we should enjoy each other's company.

Although it is common for teachers of spirituality to retreat from the world, retiring to the mountains or the deserts to do their work, Jesus preached his Gospel in the midst of daily life. And while, as a rule, such teachers take a single disciple only, our Lord addressed the masses.

He exalted collectivity. He said, 'Wherever two or three of you are gathered, I am there as well.' He prophesied the fellowship of men.

And that fellowship rests upon innocence. For where this quality is lacking, where a man or a woman says one thing out loud yet means another, or harbours undisclosed intentions towards the other, or attempts to manipulate others, to dominate others, or else is browbeaten by others, is made insecure by others—how can there be fellowship? Where relationships lack purity, how can there evolve that mood of trust, of respect and open-heartedness on which companionship depends?

Hence, even to look at a woman with lustful eyes, he said, was to commit adultery. It was a sin against our innocence and collectivity.

One day we entered the dye works of Levi. Christ looked at the scraps of cloth with which the floor was littered and said: 'Now, see.' He ordered each of us, his twelve disciples, to collect and bring him half a dozen of those scarlet, yellow, green and blue and multicoloured scraps, and taking them into his hands, he threw them in the nearest vat.

When, at Levi's direction, the workers drew them out, each and every one was white.

Then Jesus said: 'Even so has the Son of Man come as a dyer, to unify and purify.'

But we thought how men were disunited. We thought how, even though they might be seekers, they were still opposed to one another in the name of their religion, or their nation, or their sentiments, or thoughts; and while they might not spill their blood in fighting, there was still not anything resembling love. Moreover, we observed how those who followed Christ would each stress one dimension of his teaching: say, devotion to the Father, or the healing of the sick, or contemplating the beatitudes, or caring for the poor, and how already there was more than one interpretation of his meaning when he spoke about the resurrection and the Judgement, and we could see how sects were forming, with each such sect imagining that it alone was right in what it made of 'Christianity'—which, incidentally, was a title Jesus never used and would have scorned, for he taught truth, and not philosophy.

As for his statement that it were better not to see at all than to look with adulterous eyes, or that if person's right hand made him sin, it were better that he lost it, we doubted if this were not too much for men to bear.

If unity and chastity were both required before admission to God's Kingdom could be granted, how many would ever set foot in it?

We put this query to him in that dye works in Jerusalem that day.

And Jesus laughed. He pointed to the dyed white cloths and said: 'This is a time of sermons, of parables and images, and let this be one such image. But when the Holy Spirit comes with all her powers, she will throw you in the vat and draw you yourselves out all white!'

THE MUSICIAN

There was a dulcimer player whose music Jesus loved. Towards the end, when our Lord was in Jerusalem, this man would come to the house where we lodged and play to us after dark.

Long into the night he would play, until it seemed our subjection to time was dissolved, or as if across the ocean of illusion the galley-slaves had reached their port of call at last and disembarked in liberation.

After one such performance our Lord was moved to say: 'There is a left side and a right side, but this man is in the centre. There is a left side and a right one, but this man has balanced the two, and you have heard the result.

'To the left is the female, the night and the moon.

'To the left is the rhythm.

'To the left are those who live through their emotions, who comprehend relationships and understand devotion; and also those who lose themselves in their attachment to their husbands or wives or families, their tribes or their countries, and who, neglecting their seeking, cease to think of the Whole.

'To the left lies the past and Man's conditioning; to this left side lies all fear, superstition and guilt; and here live those who act like slaves.

'While to the right side is the male, the day and the sun.

'To the right side is the melody.

'And to this side go the reasoners and all who concern themselves with action; likewise those who pursue achievement, power and matter. On this side are those whose nature is ambitious, harsh or mercenary, and those who think of wealth before the heart, who place ideas above reality.

'To this side of the being lies the small and transitory self.

'But this man occupies the centre, such is the balance in his playing between technique and creativity, his passion and his reason, the rhythm and the melody, the left side and the right.

'And I tell you that to be a master of the left and the right like this, one must first have gone beyond them. One must first have become the Spirit.

'And so: when you have made the two into one, as this man has, you will have entered the Kingdom. When the female and male within you are one and the same, and the outer expresses the inner, the hands the Spirit, the eyes the Spirit, and the body in its entirety the unblemished, undying Spirit, you will have entered the Kingdom of Heaven—where absolute music is played.'

THE DANCE

We took our supper, then reclined on cushions in the house's upper chamber while our Lord spoke gravely and intensely of the Kingdom that awaited us—as though he knew his final hours on Earth had come. Then we stood and sang a hymn, after which he led us in a dance.

This was shortly before his arrest.

And in a dance of fellowship he led us, having each of us say in response to him: 'I am the Spirit, not the body; I am the Spirit, not the mind; I am the Spirit, not emotion; I am the Spirit, not the senses; I am the Spirit, not the memory; I am the Spirit, not that which suffers; for memory, mind and the body may suffer but that which stays aloof from these is not obliged to suffer, nor can it suffer, for it is joy.'

And again: 'I am the Spirit, which is joy. I am the Spirit, which is truth. I am the Spirit, which is not to blame. I am the Spirit, which is knowledge. I am the Spirit, which is peace.'

And again: 'I am homeless, yet my home is everywhere. I have no belongings, yet all the universe is mine.'

And again: 'I have no worries, yet I care for my brothers and sisters. I am free, yet of its own accord the form my freedom takes is love, it is compassion for the world.'

And through this dance in which he led us: each touching hands and interweaving to a rhythm round our Lord who himself stayed in the centre: through this dance he was seeking to show us, I believe, that his way was unconditioned. He wanted us to know it was a way of liberation, not entrapment, a way of life and truth, and not of zealotry and death.

For as a man directs a traveller to his destination, saying: 'You must go this way, but not too far, and afterwards that way, but not too far, and you had better take provisions, but not too many, in case they weigh you down; and by the following signs you will know you have reached your journey's end,' so he tried to teach us of the Kingdom. But time after time his followers would value his instruction only, not that to which it pointed, as though it were the road that mattered and not the golden city at its end. Of course, that road is to be valued: but the road he taught us was a way of life in all its wholesomeness, and not a way extracted from the whole and set apart from daily life, to which admission can only be gained when sanctioned by officialdom; a way policed by priests and fixed by articles and dogma.

His way was a way of truth and life, yet to a certain kind of mind the truth appears as dogma and life itself seems under death's hegemony. Even Christ himself they would delimit to his actions as recounted in the Gospels, even Jesus they would bind to dogma and the past. But if he let himself be bound by anything, it was by love.

And so, to show us that his way was unconditioned, and collective, and *sahaj*, he led us in a dance of joy and brotherhood and spontaneity in which, spontaneously, order arose: for the way of eternal life is not erratic or chaotic but of its own inherent nature orderly, benevolent and meaningful.

Then we went out into the night.

THE CRUCIFIXION

As they took him away to be crucified, the Roman soldiers in the vanguard asked us what kind of god would let himself be spat upon and put to death, and—as they thought—they laughed our faith to scorn.

We bore their sneers in silence...yet it was true that I had wished, in the course of that last, unending night in the garden of Gethsemane, that Jesus would call upon the powers at his disposal and rout his enemies, that his glory—and our awareness of his glory—might be known throughout the world.

I pictured legions of angels coming down from the heavens, strewing fire on the homes of the priests and on Pilate's court...and so imagining, I fell asleep.

But Jesus did not sleep, nor did he use his Father's weapons, nor did he rage against his fate. Instead, on that last, unending night inside the orchard of Gethsemane, he settled it within himself that he would not resist his destiny. And when the time arrived, he met them calmly—his betrayer and that host of elders, scribes and lying witnesses and common criminals, who were approaching in the name of Death.

In the name of Death they were coming to put him to death, because within themselves they were already dead, inside themselves they were in thrall to death.

By which I mean that those who were coming to kill him had gone beyond the margins of the left and right, and, in so doing, had given themselves to Death.

The former were those who were ruled by their conditioning, which is embedded in the past, unchanging, fixed, and therefore dead; they imposed their dead preconceptions upon the living—as when they blamed our Lord for healing on the Sabbath.

While the others were those who took the part of their small, illusory selves, thereby denying the Spirit. And as much as our conditioning is a construct of the past, so our small self is a construct of the future—since, being forever unsatisfied, it forever seeks satisfaction in time to come: it is turned towards the future and defined by that future; yet all the while the future is unreal, does not exist—it too is dead.

But Jesus was life: he was eternal life, whose domain is the present. And that is why they were coming to put him to death: because those who were conditioned lived in the shadow of the past, and the ones who were ruled by their small selves dwelt in the shadow of the future, and neither could bear it when faced with the light of the present in the person of Jesus. When confronted with that reality, alive, spontaneous and luminous, they could not bear their own unreality—and so they sought to kill him.

Again, they were coming to kill him, those envious, hate-filled men, because in going to the left, into the darkness of the past, irrationality, addiction and conditioning, they had become possessed by guilt and superstition—and by the dead—and the one who was freedom itself they could not bear. The one who was absolute logic was unbearable to them.

Men think that the powerful alone wished him dead—the chief priests, the elders, the Romans—but I remember too well that emotional, bestial crowd who took him before the High Priests; I remember the slavish and fearful, unreasoning, drunken mob who yelled for his execution while demanding release for the zealot Barabbas.

And they were coming to the orchard of Gethsemane to take Christ to his death because the ones who were identified with their small, acquisitive selves had turned their attention to matter; it was matter that occupied their minds, it was for silver that Christ was betrayed. And, since matter is inanimate, instead of saying 'their minds were occupied by matter, by property and money,' one might as well say 'their minds were filled with death'. Their attention moved mechanically, not in a living manner, not with the dynamism of love.

But Jesus was eternal life, and he came to throw open the gates of eternal life to all mankind.

Yet men crucified him. Notwithstanding his healing compassion, his impeccable virtue, they wanted to put him to death.

But to say: '*They* were evil, *they* were to blame,' is of limited value—for what of ourselves?

Every day that fight between the living and the dead, unreal and real, is reproduced in us. Every day we move towards the left or right: our attention becomes conditioned or else takes the part of our small, possessive self, and thus we deny the present, we turn away from eternal life.

This is something our priests do not see. They do not understand that in their congregations are some who, in their servility, are not unlike the ones who came in front of Pilate, chanting: 'Let him be crucified.' For the moment their unreason is put into the service of our Lord, as they believe, and their violence is subdued beneath an insipidity that they call 'Christian', but I do not trust them. Honey-tongued, they share condolences and platitudes, when what is wanted is the beauty of reality. Sugar-tongued, they dwell on death and grief—and yet the purpose of Christ's life was not to sympathise with human suffering but to help us go beyond it. They call themselves 'believers', and say they love the Lord, and think their work is God's work—yet their faith is blind and their devotion, superstition.

While there are some who go to the right, who dominate and speculate, are ambitious in the name of truth, and even use the words of Jesus as a tool to overpower the masses . . . and among them are deacons, among them are bishops and priests.

But Jesus was eternal life, and he came to crucify our own small self, our own conditioning; he came to open up in our awareness the door that leads beyond them; he came to conquer Death—and these things are what he did.

So that even while those soldiers mocked him, he was going forth in triumph.

THE WAY

Indeed, he crucified himself.

It did not seem like that, but if one knows who he was, then it follows that that is what happened. He crucified himself.

And why? To open the way to the Kingdom of Heaven. That way lies inside us, yet it was blocked by our small, vain, illusory self and all the habits and patterns and structures of our conditioning—and although a few men and women, like John the Baptist, had opened that way within themselves through their devotion and their penance, for the masses that way was as shut as with sevenfold gates of iron.

John, I have heard, said: 'Why do this work? It would be just to leave the masses to their fate, for they know nothing of the quest for truth, they know nothing of the labours one must execute to cleanse the soul—and those who do seek, they mock.'

But Jesus said: 'No. I have come to do this work and I shall do this work. In the holy land of Israel, where lies the door of the way, I shall do it; and in the city of Jerusalem, where lies the key of the door of the way, I shall do it; and by a crucifixion I shall do it, since, in this darkness, no other method will suffice.'

And in the world within he did this—while we saw a man on a cross in the heat of the day, a thief on either side of him and guards below surrounding him, in the gross, dark world without.

THE THIEVES

As for those two thieves, I think of them as like the thieves of our attention: the one like our conditioning and the other like our small, fantastic self; with Christ, placed in between them, absorbing, and forgiving, and exerting himself completely to prepare a space in our awareness to admit the grace of God.

GOLGOTHA

Did he suffer or not?

I cannot say.

I believe he did and did not suffer, that day on the cross.

The athlete's face is contorted, his lungs are spent, his muscles ache, his legs are weak, and yet his identity lies in his victory, not in his pain. Was it something like this with Lord Jesus, that day on the cross?

I, who saw him taken to Golgotha, can attest to the fact that he did not suffer as a man would have suffered—and indeed, I do not know if it is possible for the Divine to suffer as we men do, for the Divine is divine and is always divine: it knows what it is, it is truth, and truth is one with joy.

Yet how can I say that he never suffered, when they scourged his body and mocked him with a crown of thorns? Or, worse, when I saw the horror in his mother's eyes?

I believe that he did and did not suffer, there on that hill of the skull. For who would not have felt the pain of such a death? Who would not have felt its absolute humiliation? And yet the Spirit is joy, and Jesus was one with his Spirit. More than that, he *was* the Spirit. Perhaps, then, he saw his body and its torture from a distance, and within himself attended to his work: to its accomplishment and meaning. Or perhaps it was that, in the state of joy, whatever is felt is at once transformed. Therefore, it was not that he suffered, nor that he enjoyed his suffering—of course not—but that his suffering was not what we think of as suffering. Within his awareness it was changed into something else for which we have no words, for we do not know that experience.

But they are wrong—those who dwell upon his suffering and repeat in their emotions the stations of the cross; they are wrong because they do not see that Jesus underwent that death on our behalf, he played out that drama for us: so that we should not have to suffer. Not for a moment did he wish us to suffer, and that, in part, is why he accepted this crucifixion: that we need identify with suffering no longer. To imagine, then, that we should repay him by indulging in morbidity, or through an imitation of his pain, is stupidity itself. It is unwholesome and perverse. It is the opposite of what he sought.

But had these imitators been there, had they seen the crucifixion, they would know not to want to copy it. They would know that such a thing is inauspicious, that it goes against the instincts of the heart.

They think that if they reproduce his agony, if they picture his flagellation and imagine his death on the cross, if they make-believe that they themselves are undergoing it, that they are actually reliving it—all this will please the Lord and bring his grace upon them. But if they knew their Spirit, they would know it shuns such self-indulgence.

It was not a cult of suffering that Jesus came to found, but a culture of truth and joy.

JOY

Though at times he wore a robe of sorrow, in himself he was joy. Although in cursing the Scribes, he wore a countenance of wrath, in himself he was joy. Although they placed on his head a crown of thorns, in himself he was joy. Although they nailed him to the cross, in himself he was joy. Although they gave him vinegar to drink, as if they wished his last taste of this world to remind him of its bitterness, in himself he was joy. Although he died among criminals, execrated by the priesthood, spurned by the mob, and disregarded by the kin of those he wished to save, in himself he was bliss beyond all suffering; he was joy, pure joy, *nirananda*; he was love.

THE DRAMA

Nevertheless I could not bear to see our Lord on the cross, being judged and tortured by the world which should have worshipped him as its Saviour. I felt a hopelessness, I felt an anger, I felt my anger was hopeless, I felt unable to be of use, like a husband standing by while his wife is in labour, and, needless to say, I wondered how Christ's Father could allow this thing to happen. In short, I felt disheartened and confused, and having a need to be alone, I turned away from the cross and climbed the Mount of Olives.

And there I saw our Lord once more—even at the same time that, below us on Golgotha, he was being crucified. I could not speak; he greeted me; I sensed that for all my reflections on his nature I had comprehended very little of the power of his divinity.

But these days, when I tell people this, I see that few believe me. They judge Christ by themselves; they think that to him the crucifixion was what it would have been to them; and somehow they imagine that this man who was himself the *Logos*, who was born of a virgin, who healed the sick, who made whole the possessed and raised the dead, who walked on water and had in his bestowal the great gift of forgiveness, was at the same time at the mercy of his enemies, and not detached from the crucifixion but involved in it completely. Yet all the while it was his own sublime intention that he was secretly unfolding when he endorsed his crucifixion, and only incidentally that of Caiaphas and Pilate.

'For the people down below in Jerusalem I have been whipped with reeds,' he said, 'For them I shall be given vinegar to drink; for them I shall be pierced with a lance; for them I shall appear to die. But this is a drama and nothing more.

'It is a drama, this incarnation, that men may learn from the symbols I give them, and go forth in their awareness to the Spirit.

'It is a play, my life, a play of God in which I have put on a human form and acted a part in a drama, so that Man may understand he is the Spirit—and more: that he must *become* the Spirit, for the Spirit is deathless; it is love, it is joy.

'And to open the way to the Spirit so that Man may become it, I have brought about this drama of the crucifixion.

'So do not be disheartened, for without the hypocrites and Pharisees there would be no play of light and dark; without the testing in the desert, adversity and mockery, the betrayal and trial, and now this final passage on the cross, there would be no drama to behold.

'And do not fear, for what is taking place now on Golgotha is not real—not in the way that our enemies think it is real; although it is real in another way: it is a drama, to be grasped with the soul's intelligence, the wisdom of the heart.

'It is a drama, for a purpose quite other than that of which my executioners dream. They suppose they have constrained me with their law and punishment, their crown of thorns and their iron nails, their cross and the tomb they have prepared for me, but I am freedom itself, I am pure *chaitanya*—and I have come to show that this is so.

'And they think they have reduced me to passivity, when I am absolutely active in a sense they cannot see.

'They believe they have imposed their will upon me, when I am that which cannot be imposed upon. So do not you also impose your ideas or your pity on me, for I am beyond such things.

'They imagine they have bound me to that cross of matter, when I was here before the world was created, and after it has passed I shall remain. What, therefore, can they do to me?

'They believe they are putting me to death, when they are not, John, they are not, for even now to those who seek the truth I bring the gift of everlasting life.'

FORGIVENESS

Written in letters of fire on the gate he unlocked are these words: 'Whoever would enter here, must first of all forgive.'

To open that gate of forgiveness within us is why Lord Jesus came among us. Forgiveness undoes the small self. It unravels our conditioning. It overcomes the domination of those institutions. It is the key of the gate he unlocked. Of the New Jerusalem itself, it forms the ground.

But forgiveness is not acquiescence. It does not compromise with evil. When Jesus went forth to the Temple to evict the usurers, he did not pause on the threshold and say to himself: 'No, wait, I must forgive them: so I shall leave them alone.' He did forgive them, no doubt—but he fell upon them also, like a lion upon its prey.

He did what it was requisite to do, but did not weigh himself down with anger, or a brooding disquiet, or a wish for revenge. He did whatever it was right to do, and he forgave.

He forgave, but not once did he bow down. He did not say to Caiaphas, 'I submit to you.' He did not cry out for mercy to Pilate or renounce his self-knowledge. He forgave, but such forgiveness is a mark of strength and not of cowardice or powerlessness. So, caring nothing for their law or punishments, he went forth to his crucifixion in all the pride of truth.

And even on the cross he was forgiving. He looked upon the soldiers, and those sanctimonious hypocrites, the priests of the Sanhedrin who had engineered his execution, and those cruel and frivolous bystanders who for no other reason than that they wished to be entertained cried out for his death, he looked down on the city below him where the Romans—who, when all is said and done, had sanctioned his crucifixion—had already turned their backs on what was being done to the Son of Man and were feasting, and planning, and thinking of the morrow, and he said, 'Father, forgive them, for they know not what they do.' He forgave them, and likewise he forgives all men who each day take the principle of truth and sacrifice it to their arrogance and slavishness, their greed and lust.

For the moment he forgives all things except the sin against the Holy Ghost. And what he wished is that we also should forgive. He wished us to forgive ourselves, and others, and—out of courtesy—to ask our Father for forgiveness of our sins.

For: 'There is no greater weapon than forgiveness,' said Lord Jesus. 'Through forgiving you release yourselves from both the past and future, and surrender your concerns into the hands of God.'

VICTORY

Moreover, he overcame matter. For, though our Lord was perfection itself, and was made of *chaitanya*, which is the breath of the pure power of God, he had nonetheless assumed a human form, and in that form there were the subtle elements of earth and water, fire, air and ether, which are matter's constituent parts. And although matter is innocent, it has an inertia within it, and an ignorance of the Spirit—so that he who would know the Spirit must overcome matter first.

And because he had that within him which was human and material, he might have failed in his work of crucifixion. Or this was possible, yet impossible: for it may be that, to God, such impossibilities and possibilities can co-exist.

It was Mary who told us, much later, that what her son was doing was by way of an experiment, and that it might not have been successful: and I have tried to understand how this was so.

I know it was not through any weakness in himself that he might have failed, since he could not be tempted. The satanic dream of power did not attract him: he witnessed it, and let it pass. And the betrayal by Judas did not undo him: he witnessed it, and let it pass. The indifference of the multitude could not deflect him from his purpose: he witnessed it, and let it pass. The condescension of Pilate when he questioned him, the ill-will of the guards when they scourged him—when they robed him in purple and mocked him—and the scorn of the mob who reviled him: all this did not distract him; he witnessed it, and let it pass into the attention of his Father, where all that is forgiven goes. Even our lethargy as his disciples, even our apathy in the orchard of Gethsemane before they took him into custody: even that did not incline him to recede from his great work of love.

Nevertheless, he had that inside him which was human and material, and had his attention gone into his body—as they wanted it to do, when they crowned him with a crown of thorns and hammered him to the cross—had it gone into that pain, or that humiliation, or into Mary's sorrow as she stood there watching him, might he not have become enraged?

And if that had happened, what then? He might have withdrawn his forgiveness, and with a shake of his head have abandoned the world to its fate.

But this did not happen. Such was his mercy and love and self-discipline that he overcame matter entirely, on behalf of mankind. He discarded the elements one by one, as though divesting himself, in the heat of the day, of the unwanted robes he had put on at dawn, until all that was left was pure light: the pure light of *chaitanya*, the pure light of the Spirit.

And the victory was his.

THE CROSS OF LIGHT

Then, on the Mount of Olives, he showed me what in the East is called the *Adi Agnya Chakra*: and it seemed like a vast cross of light which, when I looked closer, I saw to be a human cross composed of children, men and women who, themselves, in their exuberance, seemed made of light. To either side of this cross, however, were multitudes of angry, jealous, loveless souls caught up in one or other of two vortices—one spiralling down towards a fiery darkness on the left, and the other into a whiteness, drained of all colour, all warmth, to the right.

And I heard the voice of Jesus saying: 'Those whom you see in the cross are the saved who have nurtured their own humanity, and who love me in the form of pure forgiveness, in the form of innocence, in the form of the present, in the form of truth, of the Spirit, of resurrection, or in the human form you have known; and whom I love in turn. But on the right and left are powers and places: demons, ghouls, authorities and principalities, perverse and dark activities, threatenings, wraths, sly passions and cruelties, and the hells of satanic illusion into which those who deny their humanity, and deny the Son of God, and deny the Holy Spirit, must descend . . .'

It was the Macrocosmos that I saw, at the end of the Age.

But I looked upon the sufferings of the damned with horror, and said: 'Must this happen? Must this judgement take place?'

Jesus answered my question, yet I could not quite grasp all his words, or I could not quite fathom their meaning, for this image was overwhelming and had it not been for his presence, I would have run away. But afterwards it seemed that he had said: 'This judgement must take place because it belongs to the form of the universe; it is essential to the Creation, and has been announced by the Incarnations; but as to its content—that belongs to possibility.'

Then I remember his saying: 'John, John, look after my little ones. Let them walk in the light, knowing how much I love them.'

After that I was alone again on the Mount of Olives, towards the sixth hour.

THE REQUEST

I returned to the cross on Golgotha, and Jesus, who had seemed all this while in meditation, now opened his eyes and looked about him. He saw me and his mother—who was standing close by—and spoke in a soft, commanding voice, saying first to me, 'Behold thy mother!' and then to Mary, 'Mother, behold thy son!' at which she looked at me with profound, maternal love.

This look encouraged me—for, in spite of what I had witnessed on the Mount of Olives, on seeing Jesus on the cross again I had begun to doubt our strength against the powers of evil. It was not so much the hatred of the soldiers, the priests, and the crowds that seemed so disconcerting, however, as the sight, below us in Jerusalem, of people conducting their everyday business without the least awareness of what was taking place not fifteen minutes' walk away from them. And I thought: at least the evil have their part in the drama, but these, the merely ignorant, have no role in it at all . . .

Mary now reassured me, however, for I saw in her eyes a strength I had not been aware of before, or had taken for granted; an inspiring, sustaining power not different from the power which makes the sun illuminate the world, the moon and the seasons revolve, and all living things grow. It seemed to comprehend, and penetrate, and be beyond all ignorance and evil.

So, later I took her into my care, and in time we left Jerusalem for Tiberias, on the Sea of Galilee.

But the full significance of what Christ meant, I did not realise till later.

ETERNAL LIFE

The sky became overcast. For hours on end the sky became so dark, it seemed all the light had gone out of the world. During this time our Lord's eyes were closed.

Then at last he opened them and declared in a powerful voice: 'Father! My Father! It is finished,' and his body grew limp. The crucifixion was over.

Men have said he used the words of David's psalm, 'My God, my God, why have you forsaken me?' but he did not. I was there and I can swear to this. Nor could he have said it, for implicit within such a phrase would have been a denial of what he was.

He did not say it, but men must have felt that those words of David applied to the crucifixion, and so they came, in the end, to believe that Jesus said them. Or else, because they felt forsaken, they projected all their doubts and anguish onto Christ and, in retelling the story, had him give voice to their despair.

But he could not have been abandoned by his Father because he was himself divine. Nor did he cry a cry of failure, since he had not failed. He had come to this world to open up the *Adi Agnya Chakra*, and, through the penance of the crucifixion, that was what he was achieving. Therefore, when he declared: 'It is finished', he meant not that their sentence was served, but that his task was accomplished, his work was done.

Nevertheless, the sun put on its mourning clothes of darkness while he underwent that punishment, and when he died, or seemed to die, all the elements trembled so much that a shudder ran through the Creation.

Admittedly, our Lord had warned us in advance of this event, saying that: 'The Son of Man will be delivered up for crucifixion,' but it was difficult to understand why this was happening, impossible not to feel confused, hard not to fall into the lethargy of grief—and also into anger at the ruling powers, who, it seemed, had put the truth to death. And while he had told us that no one might enter the Kingdom without being tempted first, we had expected temptation to come in the bright form of pleasure, not the dark shape of pain.

So, taken off guard, we were tempted into hopelessness.

Moreover, when we looked at his death from outside the event, Christ did indeed appear to be Isaiah's *man of sorrows*. From without, it seemed that Christ was brought down to a state of absolute submission. From without, the crucifixion both looked and was indeed a penance: a penance for all suffering, perhaps. But from within, it was a liberation from that suffering. From within, Christ was the victor, he was the joyful one, and he and he alone was absolutely not submissive to the institutions of the small self and conditioning.

From within, he was doing what he had said he would do when declaring: 'I have come to prepare the ground. In time another will come to build her palace there.' From within, he was clearing the way for us to go beyond our sins, to break our attachment to them and to break their connection to us. For we do not want to suffer, but again and again we bring about the causes of our sufferings; we veer towards the right and the left and think ourselves to be the subjects of our actions and desires and expectations, we think ourselves to be our feelings, mind and body, we think ourselves to be our small self and conditioning—and thus our sufferings ensue. We are in debt to the past in the form of the sins which, once committed, react upon us, delimiting our personalities, our lives. We place ourselves in thrall to *karma*. But Jesus unlocked the door in our awareness to the timeless present of the Spirit, beyond the reach of *karma*. By passing through that golden door we move away from *karma* to the promised land within.

And so, when he finished his work and the temple shook and the curtain veiling the sanctum inside was torn in two, it was as if to say: *now the way to the holy of holies is open to all those who seek the truth.*

But some refused the liberation Jesus offered, as though they did not want to lose their right to suffer. These were those Jews who cried out to Pilate: 'His blood be on us and our children!'—believing it a joke. I fear for them: not because our Lord will seek revenge for what they did to him, nor because his Father will punish them, but because they demanded the fruit of their actions. And what can that fruit be, but dreadful suffering?

Yet Jesus was eternal life and he offered eternal life to those who loved him. He offered it then and he offers it still and will offer it always to those who love him for what he is.

He resurrected himself in the selfsame form as before, but for those few ounces of matter that had fallen away from him, so that we could see that the Spirit is undying, it does not wax or wane, it is divine, it has eternal life.

And the rest is well known. He manifested himself among us, and I think that for the first time we, the disciples, believed that he truly was God's holy Son. Or perhaps I should speak of myself alone when I say that at last I saw the grandeur of the fact that Jesus was, and is, the Son of God.

And when I think of him after the resurrection, I seem to see him in his glory, saying: 'I am the Son of Man, I am the meaning of Creation in which every seeker may now share. I came to free you from your sins by absorbing them, and I have accomplished that. I came to curb your small self and conditioning, and I have achieved that. I came to separate the living from the dead, and see: they are separated. I came to give you the power of forgiveness, and behold, and I have given it. I came to prove that though the body dies, the Spirit does not die—and I have proved it. I came to show that truth is love—and I have shown it. I came to open the gates of eternal life—and I have done it.

'For I myself am eternal life, and when I greet you with a kiss, it is eternal life that kisses you. When I smile at you, it is eternal life that smiles at you. When I talk to you, it is eternal life that talks to you. When I chasten you, do not fear: it is eternal life that chastens you. And should you fall prey to confusion, know that I am eternal life, and it is eternal life that loves you.'

THE HOLY WOMEN AT THE SEPULCHRE

On the third morning after the crucifixion, at dawn, the women who had stood by the cross: that is, Mary, the mother of Jesus, her sister Miriam, and Mary Magdalene, went out towards the sepulchre where, scented with aloes and myrrh and wrapped around with linen, Christ's body had been laid.

Bearing ointment and spices and lilies, a lamp with which to see inside the tomb and a wreath for our departed Lord, the Holy Ghost's three forms appeared displayed in them: the maternal, sustaining, evolving form, and the form that gives comfort, and the form that gives counsel—the three forms described in India as *Mahalaxshmi*, *Mahakali* and *Mahasaraswati*, and who together, it is said, wove the world into being.

Then after some time the three Marys returned, and Mary Magdalene's cry: 'He is risen! He is risen! He lives!' pierced my being like lightning.

And here I think again of how Christ's story was symbolic, for in the Marys' presence at his resurrection there was an echo of the presence of the Magi at his birth.

And again I feel that these three women, the Mother of Christ in the centre, to her right her sister Miriam, and, to her left, Mary Magdalene, emblazoned with light and rejoicing, represented, or were, the Holy Ghost's tripartite power on Earth.

RECOGNITION

I sometimes think of the way that Jesus reappeared to us, after his resurrection. It was quietly, not brazenly, discreetly, not obviously; and though he stood within the garden of the sepulchre, and appeared in Emmaus, and walked upon the seashore of Tiberias, no one noticed him but us, no one knew him but his disciples—and even then not easily.

So, might the same thing not happen at the time of our own resurrection? That the Comforter will come discreetly, not obviously, and quietly, not transparently, and only the wakeful will know her for what she is?

'It is needful to watch and to pray,' said our Lord, that we may know her when she comes. To pray, that we may feel her love's impression on our heart; and to watch—to be alert, intelligent and wise—that we may sense her with our understanding, and not be befooled by the many false prophets who will come to mislead us.

For they will come as well, he said, and they will sell their truths for money, and people will buy them. Or they will say that the Kingdom is found on the left, or is found on the right, and hosts of people will believe them. Some will seem to work wonders or cures, and people who do not observe how their wonders are merely material and their cures ephemeral and partial, will flock to them.

And many will call themselves his followers, but he will say, 'How have you followed me? Be gone, I do not know you.'

But if we are wise and seek the truth, he promised us, we shall never be deceived.

For the Comforter will love, but not add to our conditioning. She will love, but not pamper our small self. She will love, but not spoil us. She will love and transform us.

And she will awaken within us that power by which all we need to know of what is true and what is false, of who we are, and of what the Spirit is, will be taught to us. She will lead us in the path of virtue, which is the narrow way, the lawful path, the royal road to Heaven's Kingdom. She will protect us from all evil. She will not measure out her compassion, but unstintingly pour it upon us. She will establish the New Jerusalem.

And she will take hold of our habits of mind and our small, small-minded, finite selves, and will cast them to the winds.

And we shall be soothed in her presence, and be joyful, and silent.

And in her holy presence we shall feel the Holy Spirit's holy breath, the *pneuma*, on our heads and our hands.

That is how we shall know the Comforter when she comes.

THE POWER

Jesus spoke more than once, in the days of his resurrection, of that power which is stored inside us and which in time to come will be awakened by the Comforter.

It is the pure desire of God, he said, and its nature is that of compassion. It has only one aim: that we should become what, in reality, we are already—which is to say, the Spirit—and it knows how to bring this becoming about.

It is coiled like a serpent within us, he explained, and because he had prepared us, it would ascend and bring about our knowledge of the Spirit when the time was ripe. Moreover, in the future there would be bestowed on us the capability of helping it ascend in others too.

That is what he said, though we scarcely understood it at the time, and later it was spoken of in gross and foolish terms—that now we had the power to pick up snakes with our hands and not be harmed, and suchlike nonsense.

This power he had mentioned before, but always enigmatically. 'The Kingdom of God is like a grain of mustard seed,' he had said, implying that this power was something we were simply not aware of, just as a mustard seed seems but a speck of dust until its germination.

And again, still more mysteriously: 'It is like the leaven which a woman took and hid in three measures of meal, till all of it was leavened.' And that small, hidden leaven is this rising, transforming power, and that woman is the Holy Ghost, the Comforter.

If he spoke like this, it was because he knew that we were fishermen, not scholars: our minds were too untrained, or else too obdurate, to comprehend him. Yet there was another reason also. He must have known that a man would come who would sieve his teachings for the things that did not suit his own philosophy, and reject them; and he thought that if he spoke in riddles of this power, those riddles might yet pass uncensored.

THE DOOR

Jesus said after the resurrection: 'Though in this world I must leave you, I shall always be with you in truth.'

'But where will you be, Lord?' Thomas Didymus asked.

Jesus looked at him intently and put a finger to the centre of his forehead. And then he touched me on the forehead also, and gestured at the others likewise. 'I shall be here,' he replied, 'For here, behind the eyes, is found my dwelling-place within you.

'Here is my diamond-walled palace and here is my throne-room and here I reside in the ones who accept me and love me.

'Here I work hard to dissolve your conditioning, and here your small self is dispersed through my compassion, and here I light the lamp of truth—that is, the truth that loves.

'And here is the door of the Kingdom of Heaven—the door which, by means of my crucifixion, I have now unlocked.

'But in those who slumber where the Spirit is concerned, in them I also sleep. And from those who misuse their being, who look again and again with adulterous eyes, or who do not forgive, or who create disharmony, or who are all the time angry, or who think perverse and wasteful thoughts, or who indulge in guilt or misery, or who hate their fellow men, or who are fanatics, or who think I shall act at their bidding when, in truth, they are far away from me—from them I recede.

'So, use your vision wisely, and forgive, and be makers of peace, and I shall always be active within you, here in my royal dwelling-place in the *chiasma* behind the eyes.'

This is the *Agnya Chakra*, Thomas told me later.

THE HEART

Furthermore, he told us to remain within Jerusalem—by which he meant not that city as such, but the innermost place of the heart.

To abide there, attentive; to abide there, not venturing out on the roads leading right and left; to abide there, steadfast within its walls.

Because it is there, in the heart, that the Spirit resides.

And whatever we said, we should say with the voice of the heart; and whatever we thought, we should think with the heart's sagacity; and wherever we put our attention, we should see with the eyes of the heart; and whatever we did should be done with the heart's compassion, that it might be said of us: *they themselves are the Spirit, they themselves, in their being, show forth the truth that loves.*

PENTECOST

It was the day of Pentecost, and we were gathered in a building in Jerusalem. The ten disciples and myself were there, and Matthias, Salome, Ruth, and Mary Magdalene, together with Mary, the mother of Christ. We had talked for a while of what might be done, or would could be done, or what ought to be done with Christ's work, when all at once, with quiet authority, Mother Mary said: 'Now, open your hands and be silent.'

Then something rose up through my body to induce within my mind a state of silence: a subtle, conscious noiselessness in which I felt myself at peace—a subtle, conscious stillness gifted with the qualities of wisdom and exuberance—a subtle state of witnessing in which the actions and reactions of my mundane self were stilled, with the result that, when I turned to the world about me, I felt no prejudice concerning it and no antipathy towards it, but only kindliness and love. And on top of my head I felt something moving—not something alien or strange, however, but something natural and delightful, like a flame that was dancing, like a flame without heat, or a wind that was stirring: a cool, fresh, subtle wind disporting and enfolding.

The others confirmed that they felt the same: some a little more distinctly and some a little less so, each according to their nature and condition. Also, on the palms of our hands we felt, at first, the cool, soft wind that moved within this windless room, and then faint, painless signs of fire, though no fire burned.

Now, while we were feeling these things, Mother Mary taught us that these new sensations of cool wind and fire comprised a language, and how, by using certain gestures, or by praying to Lord Jesus or the Holy Spirit, we could manoeuvre this awakened power throughout our bodies and expel the heat and cold that rested there; how those extremes expressed imbalance, dereliction, friction, sin or damage; and how this cool and subtle wind was in truth the *pneuma*, and the *ruach*, and the Holy Ghost's cool, camphor-flavoured breath.

Yet although there was not one of us who did not feel sanctified and purified, some amongst our number later fell to questioning Mary's authority and doubting what had happened. Besides, the mass of followers of Christ did not accept this new language of gesticulations: a few believed us mad and some derided us outright, while many more declared it foreign to the teachings of our Lord. At that difficult juncture such reactions unnerved us all; confused, we shrank within ourselves. And so, with the passage of time, we retained only some of those gestures and prayers, and neglected the rest; while the silent, blissful wind itself became a matter for conjecture and at length, for long periods, deserted us.

As for Mary, she did not speak in public of that cool wind again, but looked upon us, I felt, as might a mother who had tried to teach a lesson which her children were not able, or not ready, to absorb.

WORSHIP

Jesus worshipped in the Synagogue. Had he been born in the East, he would have praised his Father in the caves of Elephanta, or his Mother in the temple at Kolhapur. And had he chanced to come to Ephesus, he would have glorified her nature in the temple of Diana, since he did not scorn the kinds of worship practiced by our forefathers; instead, he came to make them meaningful. He came in order to fulfil their yearning and devotion, and not reject them altogether. So, he did not turn his back upon their temples, but entered them and sought, if possible, to cleanse them. He did not come to pit religion against religion, or insist that God must be shown homage under one name, not another . . .

But wherever God was respected, and respectfully adored, there Jesus Christ behaved as does a Son who loves and venerates his Father.

THE ROBE

But he himself belonged to no religion.

No Deacons or Brahmins were present at his birth, only wise men and shepherds; nor was he born in the temple precincts, but in a stable.

Issuing no list of statutes, he added only one commandment to those we knew already: a commandment unenforceable in law: the simple commandment to love.

And in his wisdom he saw incisively how men had gone up to the Tree of Life and picked its living flowers and dismembered its branches, saying 'This is mine,' or 'That is mine,' thereby killing what they had usurped. He saw them praising both the fragrance and the beauty of those flowers, when the flowers themselves had long since turned to dust. He saw them making weapons of the branches of that Tree with which to fight each other.

He saw how all the priests of all religions liked to clothe themselves in mystery, how they substituted signs for symbols, rote-learning for meaning, speculation for knowledge, and pomp for transformation.

He saw them for what they were. He saw their hypocrisy, cupidity, and self-deception. He stood up in the Temple in Jerusalem and poured the vials of God's wrath upon them, and in all that building not a rustle, not a murmur could be heard; the congregation held its breath; and we who knew him sat there awestruck, motionless, astonished at that purifying fury of his words.

We had said, with what we had thought was intelligence and tolerance but what in fact was only sympathy and conditioning, 'Surely there are many good men among them—surely they are good men mostly—for have they not given their lives to the service of God?' But he saw how, when the time arrived for Truth to come before them in the form of innocence and wisdom and auspiciousness incarnate, they would be the first to shout out: 'Crucify! Crucify!'

And perhaps he sensed that once he left us, his followers would disagree about his legacy—some taking the path of the Jews and some of Paul of Tarsus, some becoming ascetics and some polygamists; some turning his words into systems which they could then impose upon their converts, some intermixing his teachings with those of the Greeks or the Persians, and so on. He bequeathed his Word to all men, but for those who would contest that inheritance, who would divide or lay claim to his Gospel, or who in his name would dispute amongst themselves, he left behind, as a parting gift and symbol and also, I think, a jest, his indivisible, seamless robe.

THE PRIESTS

I ask myself what it is I do not like about the image of Lord Jesus that our priests proclaim.

Have they distorted his teaching? But they preach from the Gospels, and for the most part those Gospels contain the words of Christ.

Or is it that, when they repeat his words, they do so indiscreetly? For Christ would teach with subtle variations, or with the emphasis placed now here, now there, or would even assert the contrary, according to whom he was speaking. When addressing the faint of heart, he would say: 'I do not bring peace, but a sword,' while in lecturing the arrogant, it would be, by contrast: 'If a man should strike you on the left side of your face, show him the right side also.'

So, there is that. But there is something more about their presentation of Our Lord that I do not like or cannot recognise.

I think it is that their image lacks all *spontaneity*. It is not the living Christ who speaks when they repeat his words; it is not the living Christ they pray to, ever-present in our *Agnya*, omnipotent and innocent and wise; but a Christ forever fixed in time and place, a Christ contained within their story of his life and death, a Christ whose teachings are restricted to the few words we ourselves recorded, a Christ as static as a sculpture—and as dead.

As though they worship the crucified Christ, and not Christ resurrected.

THE PAST

And when they preach, our priests refer us always to the *past*. They say: 'As Peter stated in his letter to the exiles . . .' or: 'As Matthew wrote . . .' or—very often—'As Brother Paul asserted . . .', as though the truth is true through being written down long, long ago.

To inform their congregations of what the first disciples said is interesting, no doubt, but to repeat it endlessly subordinates the living to a text, the present to the past.

And even when they say: 'As Christ declared when he did such and such . . .' I cannot help but think, sometimes, that this too serves to draw our being to the past, to the left side, to the dead—when it is the living Christ who matters.

And even when they talk about the crucifixion, I sometimes think, 'Yes, but Jesus *did* that work. Now—what of the resurrection? What about the Comforter to come?'

EXUBERANCE

Lord Jesus was exuberant. He was exuberance himself. Though he spoke about the harvest, one sensed in him the springtime yet to come. Though he took his birth at midnight, one sensed in him the dawn, the freshness of the earth, the clean wind rising off the sea, the promise of the daylight just ahead. With him, however much he spoke of grave, important things, one could never be sombre for long; and although he proclaimed his return at the end of the age to redeem and destroy, one felt nonetheless, so long as he was near, that it was yet the morning of the world.

CONCERNING MARY

When I lived with Mary and served her as a son, in the days not long after the crucifixion, I dreamed that once again I talked with Christ. I asked if it might not be time to relinquish my care of his mother and go off instead to spread the Gospel, like the rest of the disciples. At James the Just's suggestion, I had left Tiberias for Ephesus, for fear that Mary's life might be endangered if we stayed in Galilee, but now I longed for the open road and the sea at the road's end, for a voyage to Rome, perhaps, or to ride again into Jerusalem. A restlessness disturbed me as I thought of my comrades now scattered about the world and their perilous work, their struggles and quarrels, their persecutions and triumphs. News was beginning to reach me of the labours of Thomas in far away Kerala, and I too wished to travel as a herald of our Lord. I conceived of the hearts of other men in distant lands as high-walled cities, and in my ardour I wished to storm them in the name of Jesus. Moreover, Stephen's death at the hands of Saul of Tarsus, who was active in Judea at this time, disturbed me greatly, and in contrast to the work of others, my uneventful, humdrum life in Ephesus seemed almost valueless. I believed that I should *act*, as though in action lay salvation; and the peace I had found in Mary's presence was upset by the struggle for peace in my own imagination.

And so I wished to leave, or I both wished it and feared it—and the more that I feared it, the more that I felt I should go.

In my dream I said these things to Jesus, or somehow he had access to my thoughts and knew what I was feeling, but his reply was: 'It is you who are blest, by staying here.'

'Yes,' I answered, 'but I worry that your message will be lost if we do not do our utmost to proclaim it. I worry that the seed you sowed will be destroyed.'

But he rebuked me, asking if I thought that, having once planted the seed of truth, God would then let it die? 'That seed is hidden in the earth where the powers of darkness will not find it. It is hidden in the earth within you; nor did I sow it, for it was always there, from your creation. But I have watered that ground with my blood and cleared a passage for that seed—and when its time comes to sprout, it will grow into the tree of everlasting life in those who value it and nourish it. But as for you: you cannot force that seed to grow, nor need you fear that it will die.'

'But why do you say I am blest in staying here?' I asked. 'Could I not serve you more usefully if I went out into the world and preached your Gospel?'

'Men think they are being useful to God when they stand in the marketplace, making speeches in his name, saying, "Look, the Kingdom is over here, to this side," or, "Look, the Kingdom is over there, to that side," when it would be better if they made themselves such that where they were standing, there was the Kingdom already. Do you understand me, John?'

I understood him to mean that it were better to become the Spirit than to talk about it, or that it were better to exemplify the Spirit before speaking of it. But then I asked a third time why, in remaining at home, I was blest.

And this time Jesus made no answer except to look at me intently, with a stern, lamenting gaze, at which point I awoke. And when I woke I knew who Mary was and why I was blest.

THE MOTHER

She was baking bread in the kitchen. I stood in the doorway, saying silently in my mind:

'Now I know who you are. You are the Mother of the world.

'Now I know who you are: you yourself are the Holy Spirit. You yourself are my Mother.

'Do not let me repeat this delusion in life after life, for now I see clearly that I have been blind.

'But this delusion extends everywhere; I see that now clearly, too. For I was close to you, yet far away. I have eaten your bread, yet understood nothing. I saw our Lord try to please you in all that he did, and I witnessed your pride in him; yet I saw nothing more substantial than a mother with her child. I listened, but did not hear.

'But how can this be? For I thought I knew what holiness was—yet where have I been, but at its source?

'Are you then the source of delusion as well, as they say in the East?'

And then there seemed to stand in front of me an ageless woman, untouched by time, untroubled by experience, light as air, or, no, much lighter—through whose love the world was made, more patient than stone, looking back at me, smiling. I, John, saw the Mother of Christ in a blue garment, smiling, yet with other eyes perceived the Holy Spirit, God's primal power, beyond delusion, or at the eye of the storm of illusion, smiling; and I exclaimed:

'Mother, we are children in your hands!

'Mother, we know nothing!'

THE SECRET

Three days later she left.

But before she went I asked her many things about the future and the past. Not at first, however—for at first, on the first day, I was enfolded in silence and beheld her with awe. As best I could I served her, while inwardly berating myself for having neglected her before, and for having wished to leave her.

Each time that Mary looked at me, I felt as though my soul was being taken in her hands just as a potter takes a lump of clay and turns it on the wheel. He turns it, slaps it, kneads it, gives shape to it and smoothes it off, thereby making a vessel which, when fired, can hold water. Thus was she making my soul receptive to her grace.

On the second day it was the same: a quietness filled the house and wherever Mary was a soundless wind arose, instilling silence in my heart. Then on the evening of the second day I felt I must talk, I must question her, not only on my own behalf but also on the part of other seekers, for I knew that Mary would soon take her leave. And she looked at me now not as the Queen of Heaven would, but simply as a mother, as though to give me her encouragement.

So, I asked: 'Why is it that our Lord did not declare your nature to the world?'

To which she answered, 'I would say that had you had eyes to see, you would have seen. Or had you understood who Jesus was, you would have known who his mother must be. Or had you listened with intelligence unclouded by preconceptions when he spoke of his Mother, the Holy Ghost, you would have reasoned that that eternal Mother must at the same time be this earthly one who bore him, loved him, sustained him, and took such pride in him.

'And had you really grasped what was happening at Pentecost, you would have known who this Mary must be.

'And had you understood Christ's purity, you would have understood the virgin birth; and, again, you would have seen who this Mary is.

'But as you know, you could not appreciate the nature of that birth, not really, for until Christ's resurrection you did not understand the power of the Divine, you could not accept its miraculousness. Though in the end, it is true, Matthew wrote of that birth, and Luke as well,' she said with something like a shrug; and I remembered our discussions throughout the writing of the Gospels, which Mary had overseen. I recalled how Matthew and Mark had argued, how each had stressed certain points while overlooking others, and our sense at the time that we could not convey our Lord's wholeness, nor the tone of his voice, nor his humour, his mood of meditation, or his benevolence.

'Still,' I answered, 'If Jesus had told us directly that you were the Holy Spirit, we would have tried to understand.'

'But if he had openly made such a proclamation, I would have been arrested too. I would have been charged with blasphemy. And I would have been put to death . . .

'Except that he would not have let that happen, for it is the nature of the Son of God that he obeys, protects, and seeks to please his Mother always. That is his nature: it is the very substance of his being. Had they arrested me, then, he would have used his destructive powers against them . . . and I think there would have been no end to his destruction,' said Mary, with grave finality.

There was a pause, and then she went on: 'But this would have meant that his work, his great work, would also have been destroyed; and so Jesus did not say who I was. He did not say who I am.

'But I am the Holy Spirit. I am the Wisdom of Solomon. I also was in the beginning, and am, and will be at the end. I existed before the beginning, and after the end I shall still exist. I am the primordial power of God.

'It is true: I am Sophia.'

THE HOLY SPIRIT

There was a scent of roses in the air. I knelt down beside Mother Mary and said:

'But men do not understand what the Holy Spirit is. Some say it is the Spirit by another name, some describe it as something inspiring, some claim that Jesus was the Holy Spirit and some say it is the Father in another guise . . .'

'No,' she replied, 'Men do not know very much about this Holy Ghost or Holy Spirit because they have not come near it. It is near them: in part it is within them: and yet they are not near it.

'I have heard their theories; I know them inside out,' she continued wryly, and made a movement of her hands as though she was releasing something, then let them fall back together on her lap. All this time she was sitting in a chair in the main room of the house.

'Yes: I know that some say "I like" or "I don't like" such and such, "because the Holy Spirit tells me so." But they confuse the Holy Spirit with their feelings or their reason. Or some dead thing might have taken over their intelligence, and it is that dead thing that likes, or thinks, or knows.

'Others speak about the Holy Ghost as an abstraction. They think it a neutral, impersonal entity far removed from our everyday life—or they proclaim: "It is a mystery", and so forth,' she added laughingly. 'Or they conceive of it as a dove, or something like that,' she concluded, and smiled again, and then once more grew serious.

'No, men do not know what the Holy Spirit is, but the first and last thing you must know is that it is the Mother.

'It is the Mother who has given you your existence.

'It is the Mother who loves you. It is the Mother whose love does not falter, is not possessive, is not exclusive, but is immaculate and absolute. It is the Mother in the form of infinite compassion.

'It is the Mother who wishes you to know yourself. She wants you to know what you are in truth—which is to say, in the Kingdom of God.

'And she alone is the one who can bestow that self-knowledge, that enlightenment.'

THE SECOND BIRTH

'Then it is you, and you alone, who give that knowledge which our Saviour said would set us free?' I went on.

'That is so,' said Mary in a gentle voice. 'I am the Mother who must give you your second birth. If you had understood that phrase, when Jesus uttered it, you would have seen that for there to be a birth there must somewhere be a mother. It is as simple as that.

'But this other birth is not of the flesh; it is of the Spirit and it takes place within. It takes place through the work of my reflection in your sacrum bone: through that fruitful and motherly power, when she awakens.

'Moreover, it is something *real*. You have heard men and women say, when they turn to the teachings of Jesus, "Now we are born again." But do you think that because they have said it, it must therefore have happened? If they say: "We feel we are born again," their statement is emotional; if they say: "We belong to the Church, so we are born again," their statement is merely mental—but whether mental or emotional, it has no basis in reality.'

At this point Mary leaned forward, frowned, and shook her head in puzzlement, asking:

'Yet why do they want to delude themselves? Why claim to be born again when they are nothing of the kind? Are they seekers of wisdom, or not?'

Since she seemed to require a reply, I said I supposed that they were.

'If that is so, then why should they make such claims? For while they might have changed their minds, or made some commitment to Christ, no transformation of their beings has occurred,' she continued. 'And not only is it self-deception, when they claim to be reborn although my power is still asleep within them, it is also dangerous. They are playing into the hands of forces that they do not understand.' And again she paused, leant back in her chair, and looked out into the garden, where a hawk flew among the cypress trees.

'To give this second birth is not an easy thing,' she stated quietly, as though recalling something, or turning over in her mind a phrase of poetry. 'In my heart I conceived Lord Jesus, and as a virgin I gave birth to him. That was outward; but inwardly I have conceived and given birth to you, and the other disciples, even as I did with my Son.'

Then with anxious solemnity she turned to look at me again, saying:

'But with you and the disciples it was slow and painful labour. Jesus worked and worked with you, yet still you were dull-witted and obtuse: every one of you.

'At Pentecost your second birth became complete, but still you did not accept what had happened. You were hard-hearted and recalcitrant: every one of you.

'And you are Christ's apostles. So, if you are like this, what of the others? Or is it that those who live among the mountains grow used to them, while those who see them for the first time are astonished?'

'What then is to happen to us?' I cried, close to tears.

'Do not ask what will happen to you; ask what you have to do for the world. You know what Jesus said: "You are the light of the world, but men do not light a lamp and put it beneath a bushel, they raise it up high so as to light up the house." So, let everyone know they must seek out the Kingdom of Heaven. And let them also know this: that to enter that Kingdom, they must first be born again—for they cannot go in as they are, they have to be transformed.

'And so, all those who wish to be as children in God's Kingdom—all those who wish to play within the lovely fields of eternity—must first come to the Mother.'

THE COMFORTER

Something further occurred to me, and I asked: 'Are you also then the Comforter, the Counsellor and Advocate foretold by Christ?'

And Mary said: 'I am.

'I am, for who can bring comfort if not a Mother? Who else but a Mother can heal a world split into fragments? Who should soothe you and cure you, if not your own Mother? Who knows better than a Mother how to nourish and nurture her children, and how to help them grow? And who else but a Mother has sufficient patience when it comes to guiding all her children out of ignorance to truth? Who better than a Mother to unravel your conditioning and disarm the small, false self?

'And who will take your part and be your advocate, if not your Mother? And who will be your counsellor, if not your own Mother? For she is the who will teach you the way of compassion, who will reveal you to yourselves, who will give you what you need to know—and who will at last redeem you.

'But I shall comfort you and counsel in a different form, with a different face and different name. I shall be born in another country and speak a different language; and when I come I shall come with all my powers.

'Because I have come in this life as the one who sustains: who sustains the ascent; but in that other life I shall come completely as the Mother of the world, in the magnanimity of God's compassion, in the plenitude of his love.

'I shall return in the season of judgement, both to comfort and counsel, and to awaken within my children that maternal, all-healing power by means of which the Kingdom will be theirs to enter if they wish. Yet this will happen mysteriously, as you will see . . .'

'But how will I see, Mother Mary?' I asked. 'If you are different, how will I recognise you?'

'The sunflower has no eyes, yet it turns towards the sun. The waters of the Nile have no mind, yet at Rosetta they find the sea. So do not worry, but live in the present—for it is the present that matters.

'Be brave and be humble and live in the present, for that is where joy is.

'Let the future alone, for the future does not exist. Rather, all things are contained within the present like the tree within the seed; so if you wish to know reality, to begin with know the present.'

Outside, a wind blew up among the cypresses, yet notwithstanding the fact that that was in the garden, in what was by this time the cool of the day, at sea-blue twilight, I felt it take place in my heart. I felt it happen as though the wind, the trees and the garden, and also my companions in the east and south, and the children of light beyond, and Mary herself, were contained within my heart; and there being nothing more that I could think or could say, I bowed down at her feet in silence.

THE CANDLEFLAME

That night in my room alone, I looked at the candle beside my bed and thought how the white of the flame could be likened to Jesus, while the blue burning fire underpinning the white could be likened to Mary.

He was the white flame of God who incarnated briefly in the world, intensely bright, of vivid, blazing brilliance, pointing upwards like an arrowhead and focused on a point: a task, a truth, a teaching and a meaning and the resurrection; both flamboyant and fierce, and giving off a radiance in which our souls were lit up, and our seeking ignited, and the shadows within us consumed.

And she was the cool blue fire bearing up his existence; not forward in manner but retiring; not pointing but holding, sustaining; not focused but diffused in wisdom, love and mercy; not gathering our attention to herself but in the daylight scarcely noticeable; the foundation, the root, the underlying power, the *Shakti*; the source of his compassion; blue-mantled Mary, the Holy Ghost.

While in between these two was the wick of the human soul.

KASHMIR

And so, the next day she went.

They say she died in Ephesus, but she did not. Blessing me and saying: 'We shall meet again, we shall meet when I come to awaken the world,' she turned towards the sunrise and departed.

She was going to India, to the foothills of the high mountains there, to the country called Kashmir, to meet up again with her son. For it was there that he went after greeting us in Emmaus and speaking with us later, by the waters of Tiberias. He went there by way of Andrapa in Bithynia, and Mesopotamia and Persia, and the court of King Gondapharos in Taxila; and he went discreetly, for his task in our land was complete, the drama over; he had work to do elsewhere.

As to why he chose Kashmir, it might have been because he had travelled there already, just before his ministry, and had felt at ease there, or it might have been because, after opening the gates of the *Agnya Chakra*, he wanted to prepare the path within us to God's Kingdom. And just as outwardly, in the world, the *Agnya Chakra* is bodied forth in Palestine, so outwardly, in the world, the high road to the Kingdom leads towards Kashmir.

However, it was not until long afterwards that word began to reach us of the journey he had made, and of his existence in Kashmir—and by then there were many who could not or would not accept this news. Though they professed their faith in an eternal Lord, they could not believe he was yet alive; and though they acknowledged him as the Lord of all Creation, they could not accept that he had left our land for one with different customs and another tongue.

But when Thomas returned to the West, he confirmed that these things were true. He said that Jesus was called *Issa* in Kashmir, and also *Yuz Asaf*, the 'Leader of the Healed', and that he was worshipped by some as a saint or a miracle-worker, by some as *Isa-Masih*, the Messiah, and by some as an incarnation of *Shri Ganesha*, who is God in the form of a child, and also of *Shri Kartikeya*, his warrior brother, and of the great Son of God the Father, *Shri Mahavishnu*.

And thus it was to Kashmir that Mary went—and I, John, known as the Evangelist, declare this to be true. And it was there, or in the hill country close by, that eventually she died, and there also that our Lord gave up his human form at last.

THOMAS

As for Thomas himself, he had come back, he thought, to live out the last of his years in Judea—but it was not to be so. Very soon he realised that his story of a Jesus known as *Issa*—a Jesus who was hailed as Sri Ganesha—was considered the talk of a madman. Likewise, his use of *kumkum* and oil—the one for protection, the other, baptism—was viewed as a heresy. Indeed, his continued presence amongst us was thought of by some as a threat to our faith. And as the days went by he saw he was in danger—not from the ruling powers, but from fanatics amongst our own people. Therefore, after first entrusting his writings to those who believed in Lord Jesus but who had few dealings with what had now become the one official Church, he returned to India.

I did not see him again.

And that which troubled Thomas troubles me as I speak now of these matters—for what he had seen was our priesthood assuming control of Christ's story, restricting its scope to the life that he lived in Judea, suppressing that which did not suit their purposes, and, in short, insisting it conform to a doctrine they had fashioned by themselves, entitled *Christianity*.

For example: the respect which Jesus showed to women; his talk of the secret, maternal power within us; his referring to the Comforter, the Holy Spirit, as *She*; and also Mary's role in the gathering at Pentecost—all this was being discounted, accidentally or deliberately, as the years went by.

Likewise, his acknowledging that yes, we take our birth not once but many times, was being denied, although Matthew had written clearly: 'And Jesus spoke concerning John the Baptist, "If only you can accept it, he is Elijah who was to come again."'

Equally, all talk of his journey in youth to the faraway shores of Britannia with Joseph of Arimathea, the merchant, and of his constructing a temple there: one sacred to the Holy Ghost, his Mother: was being disregarded, as was this story of his living in Kashmir—for these things could not be so simply contained by the dogma now being propounded.

But I shall speak more of this later.

IN THE CITY OF EVERYDAY LIFE

Returning to Jerusalem, I was confronted by our old predicament. We were supposed to give guidance to others, yet lacked a guide ourselves. Moreover, as apostles, we were duty-bound to spread the Gospel of our Lord, yet we did not know how best to carry out this task. Nor were we as united as we should have been.

Perhaps we had too little faith—not in our Lord, but in our own capacities.

But then, how many needed our assistance? How many clamoured for advice? Where had they gone to, the ones who had been to the mountain with Christ, the ones who had thought of his teachings as manna from heaven? Where were the crowds who had nodded their heads and agreed: 'He tells the truth, he is the Saviour'?

Some had shifted their allegiance to the cults that, more and more, were active at the time. Others whom Jesus had cured of some physical ailment were satisfied: they had no further interest in the Spirit. Still others were content with having seen the Son of God: the recollection was enough.

Further, there were those who believed that our Lord was a saint or a prophet—but that he might have truly been the Son of God was beyond their comprehension. And many were half-hearted in their seeking. On reflection, they liked it better that their holy men should be confined to long ago antiquity. The fact that generations of their forbears had revered them seemed itself a proof of holiness. And that the promised Messiah should belong to the far-distant future: this suited them equally too, since it meant that they were not obliged to ask themselves, 'Am I with Christ, or against him?'

Then, some were frightened of accepting Christ when not only had he had not received the sanction of the ruling powers, but those same powers had charged him first with blasphemy, then had him put to death. Such people knew only too well that our Lord had been crucified, and now they drifted from our gatherings and, if seen, would shake their heads and pretend they did not know us. They feared the mob, they feared the Romans, they feared the priests, they feared that others might inform on them, and, behind these other fears, they feared the wrath of God the Father—for that was what awaited those who followed Christ, according to the Pharisees. In a word, they echoed Simon Peter's error when he said of Christ: 'I do not know him, nor am I his disciple.'

Not that that discouraged Peter from denouncing their faint-heartedness in the strongest terms.

Others feared their own desire for truth, because of the responsibility it seemed to place on them. In the end, they were loathe to break with their conditioning, or they preferred their own small self's small dreams, and—like the Gaderenes, who had seen Christ's power yet who had still entreated him to leave their neighbourhood—these men were frightened at the thought of holiness, were frightened at the thought of God. The grandeur of these things was far too much for them; to some degree they sensed who Jesus was, but stronger than that recognition was their wish to lead small, simple lives untroubled by such matters as the war on evil and the quest for resurrection.

These doubts and fears infected us as well. I cannot pretend they did not. We had known our Lord, not for a lifetime, nor even since our childhood, but for three or four years only. And now he was gone, and those few years of our intense belief in human possibility seemed but the flicker of an instant when compared with all the centuries in which Man's inner life had stayed unchanged.

To conclude, then: there were many in the darkness of this dark world who were anxious to hear stories of the light, yet few who grasped the meaning of those stories and fewer still who were prepared to seek that light within themselves. There were many simple-hearted men and women who were eager to be told about a Kingdom waiting for the meek and humble, yet few were brave enough, athirst enough, or wise enough, or well enough equipped, to travel to that realm inside their being. They were content to be the faithful ones, to have a God to whom to pray, to have their lives shored up by a belief that one day soon, though not quite yet, their lot would be transformed. And, being used to masters, governors, and tetrarchs and the like, they recognised the mystical, transcendent Son of God more easily than they understood the Son of Man.

It was to these, the virtuous whose seeking was not yet fully grown, that Christ had bequeathed his parables—those riddles growing in the mind like living things.

And then, what could I tell them of Mary? For that matter, how could I speak to my fellow apostles of what I now knew about her? Thomas was in India, and as for the rest, I could not be sure of their response. Peter was, of all of us, the most resistant to the notion that as far as our spiritual work was concerned, a man's and woman's functions weighed the same; he made the point repeatedly that Christ had chosen only men as his apostles—while as for Mary Magdalene, he still considered her unclean. So: would he now accept that Mother Mary was the incarnation of Almighty God's sustaining power? I feared he would deny it. Besides which, somewhere Mary still resided in this world, and I could not let myself say anything that might endanger her.

It was as if I were a man who, having travelled abroad on a perilous journey, has now come home again—but instead of the welcoming faces and the joyful reception he had hoped to find, meets only with strangers, indifference, and silence.

I acted like somebody lost in the streets of the earthly, material city, bemused by all the sights and sounds around him. Enchanted by the music of the flute girls and the hot wind spiced with perfume from the incense trees and flowers, he wanders through the royal pleasure grounds entranced, or else his attention is squandered in worry—and money, food, shelter, the future, obsess his thoughts; his eyes are pulled this way and that like those of country boys in the bazaar; he squabbles with his friends and, caught up in arguments about who does and does not have authority, he no longer trusts himself—in short, his senses are bewildered by the world's complexity. And this was true of all of us. So that often it seemed that the watchman had fallen asleep while the long night was passing and our boat had slipped free of its moorings—and now, beneath the faint, dissolving stars of morning, we found ourselves far out to sea, no land in sight, upon the ocean of illusion . . .

PAUL

And then there came into our midst a man called Saul, or Paul.

We knew his story by report. This was the man who, soon after the resurrection, had waged a campaign of destruction against us. This campaign was partly intellectual: Saul would argue with and ridicule Christ's followers at every opportunity. Yet violence was involved as well. To Saul, our Gospel was not merely false, it was political—and if allowed to spread unchecked, it could lead to revolution. 'You have killed the head, but not the body,' he told the Pharisees, 'and now from that body a thousand heads have grown. We must act with decision and speed, before it is too late.' So, with other bigots of his kind, he raided our homes, confiscated our goods and arrested our people.

Moreover, he was the one who had egged on the rabble to murder Stephen.

Then, something unexpected happened. Saul was travelling to Damascus with letters of authority signed by the high priest in Jerusalem in the hope of stirring up the ruling powers against our brethren there, when he had an accident. According to the story, his eyes were blinded by bright, flashing lights while a voice asked what he meant by persecuting Christ. And at this, he became converted to our faith. Looked after in

Damascus by a man called Ananias, he undertook a course of study in our teachings and assumed a new name: Paul. Then he started preaching, and shortly afterwards came back in secret to Jerusalem. However, being neither trusted by the Christians nor accepted gladly by the Pharisees—who now considered him a traitor—he quickly left again for Tarsus in the north, his birthplace in Cilicia.

Eventually, he reappeared in public and began converting others to Christ's Gospel in Arabia. And now, some three years after his adventure on that journey to Damascus, he was arriving in Jerusalem, to meet with the apostles.

But there was more. It was said that this Paul was endowed with great gifts of the Holy Spirit: he could speak in strange tongues, had visions, and was in communication with the Lord. And by the laying on of his hands, his gifts of prophecy could then be conferred upon others, so that they could also utter mysteries of the Spirit.

Those who had told us these things were not insincere, we knew some of them well, and they had witnessed these gifts for themselves. Moreover, they asked if this was not the greatest of Christ's miracles: that he who in the past had been the chief among our enemies was now our foremost friend.

So, Paul was approaching us now in the manner of one who turns up at the court of a king when that king has just died, saying: 'I too am his son, these and these are the proofs. Now, give me what is mine.'

THE MEETING IN JERUSALEM

But we were not a court, nor was the king dead.

I think that all of us viewed this man Paul with suspicion, some more and some less, but none of us voiced this suspicion—for none of us wished to be thought unforgiving or jealous. Besides, all around us, amongst our friends and in particular among the newer followers of Christ, there was excitement at Paul's arrival and much talk of his conversion—and of our Lord's instruction to forgive our enemies.

And so, when Paul arrived, our brothers made a great display of hugging him—while to our sisters he seemed like the lost sheep of the parable, the one over whom the shepherd rejoiced so much when he was found.

I saw all this, but I could not find it in my heart to celebrate or overcome my doubts. I smiled too, but not within myself, and those who knew me chided me and questioned my reserve.

As for Paul himself, he was not as I had imagined. Instead, he was a small man with an unbecoming countenance—and I saw that others thought this too, and that accordingly they showed an even greater fondness for him, since he was neither handsome nor seemed gifted with good health.

Also I noticed how forceful he was in his speech and his movements, and how his comrades looked upon him as a prophet, to be revered.

Now when, years later, Paul wrote of this time, he swore that he only met Peter and James. It is true that he met with Peter first—in fact, he spent some days alone with him—but then he encountered the rest of us too. Yet: 'I saw none of the other apostles except for James, the Lord's brother. In what I am writing to you, before God, I do not lie!' he told the Galatians later—protesting, I think, too much. Though it might be that by then he had forgotten us, for with our reticent manner we might not have impressed ourselves upon him—might not have answered to the busy, martial image he had formed as proper for Christ's men.

What then? We dined together to mark Paul's coming, and from all sides the talk flowed freely. But I noticed how little he ate and how little, at this time, he spoke. In comparison with him, we must have seemed gluttons and windbags, insufficiently serious, too playful by far. And after we had retired, he and his party prayed long into the night.

So, when we gathered in private on the following day to discuss his ideas, I think that we, the apostles, felt put to shame. Here was a man who had been very far from Jesus, had been converted through a vision, and was now in earnest about our work; and we reflected: see how far he has come, and where are we? What have we done with our lives? What are we doing to please our Lord?

Still, Paul's particular concern seemed insignificant to us. His argument was that those amongst us who were Jews should sever their connections with tradition and eat with non-Jews. This latter wish was Paul's especial hobbyhorse: he was riding it then, and many years later, when he fell out with Peter in Antioch, he was riding it still. It may have been because he was a Jew himself, a Pharisee, and had given so much of himself in the past to the Jewish idea, yet in vain, that now he was keen to confront this Jewish law. Indeed, he talked as if the Jews alone were guilty of Christ's crucifixion.

'But the Romans are in power in our land,' Philip countered, 'And it was they, in the end, who put Christ to death.'

Or the Romans and Jews in collusion, he might also have said: with the former representing Man's small self, and the latter his conditioning. Though all things being equal, it was true: the Romans had the power, and therefore it was they and they alone who made the crucifixion happen.

But Paul pared the matter to the bone, heaping argument upon argument, now citing the prophets, now citing his own example, now seeking to justify himself, now appealing to God and to Jesus—or, as he called him, 'Christ Jesus'—while all the time a pair of his confederates sat next to him in silence, observing his effect on us.

Yet in his manner I saw nothing of the carefree gravity of Jesus, nor did he speak even once of Christ the man, or of his compassionate power, or of the forgiveness of sins, or the Heavenly Kingdom within us.

Then James said: 'You would have us change men's souls from the outside, by altering their customs. But let their souls be transformed first, and the customs will follow.'

This did not satisfy Paul, however, and I began to think: he considers us his rivals, for that is how his mind works. The axis that it turns round is one of power, and not of love. Therefore he would have his followers imagine that—in contrast to him—we have failed to throw off our Jewish way of thinking and remain instead committed to what he calls 'the circumcision party'.

But this was not so. When he wrote to the Colossians that 'here'—among Christ's people—'there cannot be Greek or Jew, circumcised or uncircumcised, barbarian, Scythian, slave, or freeman, but Christ is all, in all,' he was only saying what we knew already and what we had, as far as we were able, put into practice. Though we were not going to tell the Jews: 'You must give up your heritage first, before you can come to Christ,' anymore than we were going to tell the slaves: 'You must *first* of all be freed, and *then* you may come to Christ.'

But this approach was not enough for Paul, who urged us to use our powers as apostles as he was using his, to spread the Gospel more forcefully.

Then James replied, 'But you are not an apostle,' by which he meant that Christ had not himself made Paul his messenger. To which Paul returned that, no, he was not an apostle as we were. Nevertheless, he *was* an apostle—since he had been appointed by Christ Jesus in a vision, and this must be accepted. For observe, he said, what work he had done already, how much he had preached, what pains he had suffered, and how many churches, or groups of Christians, he was establishing in Antioch and Cyprus. The proof was there for all to see. Sinner that he once had been, the Lord had chosen him, forgiven him, and conferred on him the title of *Apostle to the Gentiles*.

He did not say, as he was to say later, that the Lord had set him apart for this task even before he born; he merely stated that the Lord had chosen him in spite of all his sins as a sign to unbelievers.

But now I saw something else. I saw what his purpose was in grouping us together with the Jews.

He wanted his own constituency. He wanted that we should take Christ's message to the Jews, while he would take it to the Gentiles—which is to say, to the whole world outside our homeland.

And Peter accepted this.

But we said that Christ had not made us apostles to the Jews alone, anymore than he himself had taught or healed or blessed only Jews, and no others. He had been born a Jew among Jews, of course—but whom had he excluded from his company because they were not a Jew? Did he say to the crowds who followed him into the hills above the Sea of Galilee, 'Be gone, all those who are not of Jewish blood'? On the contrary, he shared his wisdom with all those who listened. He preached the Gospel of the Kingdom to the children of the light, whether they were Jews or Greeks or Romans, or men from the East or the South.

The centurion whose servant Jesus healed was a Roman, not a Jew. And the woman in Sidon whose child he cured was a Greek, a Syrophoenician by birth. And when he directed us, after the resurrection, to be his witnesses, he told us to go not only throughout Judea but into Samaria too and beyond—to the ends of the Earth, indeed.

As for the Jews themselves, had he not reserved his greatest scorn for those who conflated truth with Jewish custom and believed themselves to be the guardians of truth? And had he not grown tired, sometimes, of the way we would search out the psalms and the prophets for intimations of his life, when he was there in person before us? So that when we said: 'Twenty-four prophets spoke in Israel and all of them speak in you,' he replied: 'You have omitted the one who is among you and spoken but of the dead.'

All this we explained to Paul, but he paid it no heed. Instead, he passed on to the question that had occupied us all since Christ had left us: the one great question of that time: how to organise his followers.

THE CHURCH

This matter weighed on James in particular, because it was to James that the stewardship of the work had been entrusted; but all of us were concerned with it, all of us were anxious that the form into which we cast Christ's followers should endure, yet at the same time not constrain those followers. That there had to be a form we accepted, for if we did not mark off our field in some way from the wilderness, it would soon revert to wilderness, or so we feared, and within a generation, Christ's Gospel might be lost.

Besides, we had to preserve that Gospel's purity—for, on the one hand, malevolent souls were spreading wild rumours as to Christ's behaviour when amongst us, while, on the other, sick or self-punishing individuals were coming forward, claiming visions of Jesus, alleging he had called on them to suffer for the world, or declaring that they had in their possession secret teachings not yet known to his disciples. This talk had all to be countered and the truth about Jesus established.

And so, we wrote down his story and teachings in a single collective book. This we did under Mary's supervision, shortly after the Resurrection.

And because people wanted a form in which to worship Christ, we composed a simple service based on the form and image of his last supper with us, we sang the hymns he had loved, recited his prayer to the Father, told stories of his life, ate bread and sometimes danced together.

Moreover, we had to ensure that we kept in touch with each new group of followers and that these groups had guidance, so we positioned men and women on whom we could rely as these new groups' advisors.

But we were averse, by nature, to the business of planning and organisation, and the construction of officialdom. Besides, we remembered too well the burning words of Jesus when he criticised the Scribes and Pharisees for the way they sought to dominate the masses.

That was the time when he warned us to call no one *Rabbi*, as we had but the one teacher: God.

Whenever we travelled with Christ as disciples, we could see that the manner of organisation that leaders impose upon men and events, which is stratified in orders and degrees, which conditions, and which petrifies, was of no use or interest to him. Rather, his behaviour was spontaneous. As the situation was, so he managed things accordingly, and because his manner was auspicious, so doors were opened, storms dispersed.

With Jesus, all organisation served the Spirit, not the reverse.

It was his teaching that what is living knows how to organise itself. To the sycamore Man does not have to say, 'Grow like this,' for it grows by itself without thought. Nor to his body does Man have to say, 'Grow like this,' for it grows by itself, without thought. Nor need the child in the womb declare, 'I shall have for myself two eyes, two arms, two legs, and so on,' and yet it happens all the same.

And that occurrence is God's work.

But when it comes to how he lives his life, Man feels bound to say, 'I shall do this, I must do that, and this will happen, and then I shall do such and such' . . . and so subordinates what is living to his thoughts, which are lifeless in themselves.

And if things happen as intended, he is not surprised; while if they happen otherwise, he is upset. Thus the wonderment within him at this great Creation dies. His life is haunted by his plans, his hopes and fears, and anxiety overwhelms him.

'So, take no thought for tomorrow, for the morrow can care for itself,' said our Lord. 'Rather live in the present, in the presence of God.'

These precepts we tried to uphold, neither impeding ourselves nor encumbering others with excessive injunctions, procedures or systems. In any case, to what extent were we supposed to organise Christ's followers? Was it our task to establish God's Kingdom? No, not exactly, for that Kingdom existed already. Nor did we control the road to it. We could only say: 'There is a kingdom; it lies beyond the seven seas within us; it is in, and yet not of, this world; it can be reached by the blest in a moment of time; it is a kingdom where fellowship reigns, a place where men are acquainted with joy as, here, they breathe the air; its topography has been described by Christ; its gateway has inscribed on it, "Welcome, welcome, welcome are the innocent!"; its gateway is guarded by angels; nor can it be found out by thinking, or feeling, or by cunning, or force; it is the country of reality; the place of eternal life.'

We knew also that the work that Christ had done was by no means the end of the matter. He had opened up the narrow way within us, but had not yet brought us to our destination. He had opened the Agnya Chakra, but not yet the Sahasrara placed above it. He had sown the seeds, but had yet to harvest them.

Our role was to see to the growth of those seeds, as far as we were able, and prepare the field for the Harvester—who is the Comforter to come.

So, all in all, we were reluctant to involve ourselves too much in organising and controlling.

But Paul would have none of our scruples. He urged that we move with greater expedition, not only founding churches but also instituting priests, who would supervise the moral life of those in their congregations, in addition to preaching the Gospel. They would be there to keep order and have the power—under our authority, that is—to expel the unworthy and cast out backsliders.

Paul had once been a soldier, it was said, and here he spoke of a soldier's objectives and tactics.

And if *we*, the rightful ones, did not construct this Church of Christ efficiently and firmly, he said, then others would—and not, perhaps, as we would like. This argument, I saw, weighed heavily with Peter. But I was troubled at this—as also were Philip and James, my brother. On the one hand, we felt chastened by the presence of this man who, by the testimony of others as well as of himself, had done so much—and in so little time—to carry Christ's work forward; yet, on the other, our hearts were not delighted by his being with us, our minds were far from soothed.

Then James led us all in prayer, after which our visitor departed.

RUMOURS

He set out for Cilicia, far away from us.

Meanwhile, our work in Jerusalem met with further opposition from the Jews—and, just as our Lord had predicted, we were barred from the Synagogue. Worse, there were arrests under Herod Agrippa, and my beloved brother James was put to death. In short, we were ground again between the mills of power and superstition—between the great *I am* of Rome and the vast *It is, it has always been* of our own Judaic tradition.

And all the while reports would come to us that Paul of Tarsus was abroad, carrying missions to Greece, to Cyprus and to Syria. And it was said that he preached a strange gospel: not the Gospel of Jesus, but one of his own.

At first we discounted this rumour, since it could not be denied that he was praising Jesus as the Son of God and, ostensibly, was labouring in his name. This was a season of magicians; of dreamers and seers and outlandish religions; of fanatical men who proclaimed that the end of time was come; of false teachers and false Messiahs—and undeniably Paul spoke of Jesus, the Son of Man. Besides which, true seekers were coming to us through having first encountered Paul.

Also, we discounted this rumour because ours was an era of rumours, and we who bore witness to Jesus knew only too well the harm that rumourmongers did.

Again, Paul was now working with Peter—and this seemed to give validity to everything he did.

For my part, I thought little of this rumour for the very reason that I wanted to believe it: because I had no love for Paul. His person and his manner had not served to recommend him to me, nor had something in the way he spoke of Jesus: an abstract, sharp impersonality. Yet, not wishing to be thought ungracious or, as we say these days, 'unchristian', I sought to overlook these things.

And then, we failed to conceive of anyone opposed to Christ proclaiming Christ, hence we put this rumour to one side. True, we had had experience of Judas, but he had been a taciturn and inward-looking man, quite unlike Paul; moreover, he had been a friend of sorts, who only at the end had changed into a traitor. But now we were confronted with an enemy turned friend, and that was another case entirely. Paul had been a violent enemy, bringing murder upon us—yet, strange to say, it was the very violence of his opposition that, for many of our number, made his subsequent change of heart the more commendable, and they followed Paul's own argument: that through forgiving his sins, the Lord had shown mercy to all.

In addition, many friends of ours admired Paul's energy in spreading the word of Christ—and when they compared his results with ours, it was not to our advantage.

I too had respect for his energy, but whence it came and to what end it pointed, I did not know.

THE ACTS

The years went by, and what had been rumours turned into stories, and stories at last became facts. Witnesses of Paul's activities in Greece came forward; some whom he had expelled from all communion with Christ spoke out; Mary Magdalene and others among the women protested; and lastly his writings appeared—and the gospel he preached was plain to see.

I speak here, of course, of things that happened long ago, and with this advantage: that now I have read a number of Paul's letters, together with the book called *The Acts of the Apostles*, whereas I think that then we only knew his letter to the Romans. But my feelings today have not changed, they have only grown clearer.

Now, *The Acts of the Apostles* is thought by some to be the work of Luke—but in truth it was written by Paul. The beginning was written by Luke, perhaps, but the work as a whole, its content and orientation, is that of Paul alone.

True, there are those who have heard this assertion, yet insist upon Luke as the author because the book begins with the device of an address to one Theophilus, as Luke's own Gospel does; but such people ignore the substance of the book. They ignore the material. Here we learn nothing of

Jesus the man, while as for the ones whose adventures the book claims to tell, they are first presented as a brotherhood of mediums, quite unlike the men whom Luke described, and are then excluded and forgotten. It is Paul of Tarsus who takes precedence, it is Paul whose eulogy the book becomes.

Luke was a doctor and painter, a man of art and science, not an author of tall tales and lies. But Paul—Paul falsified the truth at will. He cast himself as hero of the story that he tells, so that now his name is taken as a blessing and his inventions are thought of as facts.

Even when he speaks of his conversion he cannot quite be trusted. Three times he tells this story. In one version, he is merely told to proceed to Damascus. In another, the Lord explains that there he will be told of what it has been prearranged for him to do. And in the third, while Paul lies dumbstruck on the ground, Lord Jesus gives a speech, engaging this fanatic as his envoy to the world.

See too how he describes the day of Pentecost. The advent of the Holy Ghost in our awareness—that beautiful enlightenment—is told as if it brought about a kind of lunacy. He has it that we spoke in tongues we did not understand to people whom we did not know, and he ascribes this madness to the Holy Ghost.

There is no truth in this. What he describes is something I have often seen in those who wander from village to village and call themselves prophets, in witches and counterfeit healers, and also in some of the sick who came to Jesus. It is a possession by dead spirits. It is a state in which the soul is overshadowed by an entity, and not the soul but the entity speaks, not the man but the ghost shouts or cries. Such a thing is no gift of the Holy Spirit, as Paul asserts, but a gift of the dead. Neither is it a gift, I should say, but a loan to be repaid with interest. For the man who invites the dead inside himself must bear their weight upon his back, must expedite their wishes, and must, at length, have cause to suffer—for what is he doing but accepting death?

All of which is clear enough, if we look at the thing with discretion. For a man to speak in foreign tongues he does not understand is of no use to anyone. And if sometimes it happens that a man or woman, standing by, should understand what he says, or if the entity within should speak his own language—which effects Paul describes as *prophecy*—we should know that what comes from the dead is death. Those entities are not the dead who abide in the heavens, but those who linger in this world, neither fully accepting their death nor retaking their birth, but existing through others. They are shadows of varying quality: some of them are meddlesome and some depraved, some are evil, some ambitious, and some are hungry for release.

They are the spirits whom Christ cast into fire or water, in order that the living human bodies they had dwelt in might be free of them and their own unhappy personalities be dissolved among the elements—that their souls might take their birth anew. Once, he put them in a drift of swine, which then ran headlong into the sea. Yet, regardless of this, there are still those among us who summon these entities into themselves in the name of Christ, and think that in being possessed they have done something great, have achieved something holy. And the instigator and chief practitioner of this occult accomplishment was Paul. It is there in a letter to Corinth: how he boasts that, of all those in his circle, he is most prone to this speaking in tongues. Thus he makes of his affliction something marvellous, and then, to go further, writes that we who were gathered with Mary upon that day of Pentecost were subject to possession too, according to the model Paul embodied.

To present this behaviour as the Holy Spirit's work is nothing short of blasphemy. Does the Holy Spirit wish to make men idiots? Or is she trivial, or erratic: now uttering banalities, and now dictating nonsense? Are we to suppose that Jesus came to put men into trances, or to make them cry or moan involuntarily, and to rob them of self-mastery, or have them sweat and dribble in the midst of others, proclaiming gibberish?

He came to exalt the Human Being, not to have men be like animals or fools.

Besides which, there are migrants and scholars who know many languages, and this is not uncommon, but what the Holy Spirit has to give us must be something rare and wonderful.

Although some sixty years have passed, I can recall that moment in Jerusalem as though it were an hour ago. I remember Mary: her authority and gentleness. I remember the *pneuma* and the music of silence. I remember that all of a sudden I saw how it is that the Kingdom of God is eternally present within us, as Jesus had said, while being both hidden and yet to come. It is a dimension of our awareness, and the day will come when those who seek the Kingdom earnestly, wholeheartedly, will enter into it *en masse*.

I recollect as well how Mary tried to teach us that the *pneuma* constitutes a language through which all men may be understood—not in terms of what they say, but in terms of their nature: for the words of our mouths are relative and transitory, but our inmost nature, which declares itself through words of wind and fire, is not. To the man who hears this language, all men speak in words of fire and wind, and through that unerring sacred wind he can speak in turn to them, to their souls, and soothe them and cure them, although they do not hear him with their ears. But among the ones who know their own selves well, soul talks with soul in this language; soul speaks to soul in this parlance of love.

However, we neither valued nor completely understood our Mother Mary's teaching, nor would Peter acknowledge her right to teach us—and so of that event there remains now very little: some fragments in my memory, in one or two men's tales, in the gestures still used in the Church—and in the Pentecostal story reinterpreted in the *Acts*.

THE POPE

As to the picture he gives us of Peter: this is a Peter refashioned by Paul. His dreams have been made into visions, his speeches have now become lectures, the Christians who helped him are transformed into angels, and so on. The Peter known to me was not like this.

What is striking in these *Acts*, however, is the way that Peter is the one marked out by Paul as chief of the apostles. It is *his* deeds that are mentioned, *his* words that are quoted. But while in his outgoing way he was often our spokesman, and it was he who had seemed most at ease with Lord Jesus, asking questions at will, he was nevertheless not our leader. As I have said, the recommendation we had had from our Lord was that, in case of disagreements, we should consult his brother, James. But that there should be a *leader*: this too was Paul's idea, not Christ's—for Jesus would never have taken a single human being, with all his fallibility and partialities, and made him leader over all the rest.

'But is it not written,' say our priests in reply, 'that Christ himself chose Peter? Is it not written that Christ declared to him, "On this rock"—meaning Peter—"I shall build my Church"? Was it not into Peter's hands that the keys of the Kingdom of Heaven were placed? And did not Matthew, the apostle, report this?'

Yet Matthew wrote no such thing. What the Christians of this present time do not know or have forgotten is that once he had established his authority, Paul sifted through our Gospels for the things that did not please his rational philosophy. Of course, he gave his reasons. He argued that our versions of the Word of Christ must be coherent, and that anything strange to the mind—to *his* mind—should also be excised.

I was not present, but I know how Matthew answered. He said that Jesus did so many things, and that each of those things had so many dimensions, that there could never be one final gospel summating, explaining, and exhausting his work. But Paul wanted order. He wanted a text on which he could then build a Church. He wished to limit the unlimited.

In particular, he could not accept the virgin birth. Why? Because he could not understand it. Its purity and poetry were far beyond his rationality. So, he ordered both Matthew and Luke to delete their account of it. However, they resisted him.

Nor could Paul appreciate the nature of Christ's miracles—since, do what he might, he could not be cured of his own affliction. Nor could he accept the fact of that maternal power within us that will bring about our second birth by ascending and piercing the fontanel bone, thereby baptising us truly. He feared, I think, that if this were known, it would render null and void the baptism he conferred within his Church—which was only material, which was only external. Thus, as far as he could, he omitted Christ's teaching about it.

Nor was he willing to let there be much said of Mary, Christ's mother. He could not understand the respect with which we treated her, for as he wrote to Timothy, 'I permit no woman to teach or have authority over men.'

Nor was Paul pleased by allusions to the Comforter, since she did not fit into his scheme of things.

More than this, though, Paul interpolated certain passages in the Gospels. Jesus did not say, 'Who is my mother, and who are my brothers?' but only: 'Who are my brothers and sisters? Here are my brothers and sisters! For whoever does the will of God is my brother or my sister.' Nor did I write that Jesus said to his mother in Cana: 'O woman, what have you to do with me?' for Jesus would never have said such a thing. No-one could have shown their mother more solicitude than Jesus showed his mother, Mary. And it was Paul, perhaps, who had him ask on the cross, 'My God, my God, why have you forsaken me?' in order that his recognition of our Lord as the Messiah would seem the more significant. If Jesus was the King, then Paul at least could be the kingmaker.

And it was Paul, for certain, who had Christ declare that Peter was the rock on whom he would construct his Church.

PETER

Yet Paul could never have said this had it not been with Peter's consent. To go further, his work as a whole would in no way have been so effective, had Peter not assisted him.

Paul must have sensed, soon after his conversion, that his case for being Christ's apostle to the Gentiles lacked sufficient weight—however much he spoke of being chosen in a vision. Those who knew Christ's story well would not respect him in the same way they respected us, who had known our Lord in person. Nor, at that time, was he the sole pretender to the title of 'apostle'. And so, he must have reasoned that in order to succeed, his work would first require the sanction of the true apostles—or, if not of all of them, of one of them at least.

Accordingly, before we met him in Jerusalem, he had his agents sound us out. And on the basis of their reports, he must have come to a decision. He would go to Simon Peter first.

He had known his man. It had rankled with Peter that James—that sober, judicious, undemonstrative man—should have been accorded precedence over him in this matter of spreading the Gospel, when he himself, he considered, was by far the more capable. *He* had no self-conscious diffidence, was not impaired by hesitancy; was outspoken, outgoing. Yet he was also prone to anger, wanting in diplomacy and overly impulsive, and altogether he lacked that subtlety of character through which the Spirit most effectively conveys itself.

But Paul assured him that, in his own and others' eyes, he was the principal apostle, and that therefore—for Christ Jesus's sake—they should labour together to build up the Church.

And Simon Peter agreed. He was spellbound by Paul's decisiveness, by his ability to organise—and by his flattery.

As for his being 'the rock' on which Jesus would found his Church, Paul must have convinced him of this. He might have said, 'Look, friend, in naming you *Cephas* or *Peter*, Christ Jesus was telling us something. He was saying that *you*, and you alone, are that rock on which the wise man's house was built—the house of the parable, which stood upright for all the wind and rain.' For Peter was not like those other apostles, Paul would have gone on to add, who seemed composed of sand—the sand on which the foolish man's house was built. No, Peter was strong, he understood the need for order and authority, he was by virtue of his temperament a leader over men. Then Paul would have said that the house built on rock was the *Church*, and that what Christ had intended was that Peter should be its first leader, its *father*.

Paul would have said this because, for him, the end legitimised the means. And out of vanity, ambition and self-deception, Peter must have said, 'Yes, it is so.'

Yet the purpose of Jesus was never to build any Church, but to open the gates of Heaven!

Of course, I know that when I say these things of Peter, many shake their heads and look askance. To say that Paul was in reality against us: that is already too much; but to add that Peter was corrupted by his vanity . . . they think I have some score to settle, or that the Gnostics have worked upon me. They think there must be something to the story Paul put about: that *John can no longer be trusted—has some sinister motive for what he maintains—has become a heresiarch—perhaps an antichrist.* And were I not an old man, and therefore one whose recollections and avowals, if thought to be too awkward, can be dismissed as wanderings, I might have been shunned by my brothers and sisters long ago.

Yet it is true. Peter allied himself with Paul, and in place of Christ's living truth they put an empty tomb, mistaking the one for the other.

I do not say this of Peter with anger, although I should feel anger, but rather with pity. He had much within him that was great, and it might have been that, had he trusted to his Spirit, he could have built upon that greatness—for did not our Lord remark that: 'I have prayed for you, Simon Peter, that your strength may not fail'? Indeed, it might have been that, in his faith, he could have become as a rock: with that same unwavering stability. But in the end he took the part of men, and not of God. In the end he let another gird him and direct him in a way he would have spurned, had he retained his wisdom: and that other one was Paul.

To those who question this, I ask: to whom did Jesus say, 'Get thee behind me, Satan'? Was it not to Peter? And of whom was Jesus speaking when he said that Satan had demanded he might have him, in order to sift him like wheat? Was it not of Simon Peter? And of whom did our Lord say, 'O man of little faith', when that man fell into the waves? Was it not of Peter? And were those waves not the waves of illusory, everyday life and its fleeting, unavailing desires? And which of us denied our Lord not once, not twice, but thrice before the cock crew? Was it not Peter? And to whom did the risen Lord say, with an insistence that the other did not understand—not merely once, nor twice, but thrice—'Do you love me?', then adding the injunction, *'Follow me'*? Was it not to Simon Peter?

In spite of his physical strength and in spite of his feeling for Christ, he was weak, and this weakness derived from his vain, small, resentful self—which was indeed like a rock. And notwithstanding the fact that Paul took hold of them and altered them, that weakness is there in the Gospels: it is noted down clearly for those who wish to look and draw their own conclusions.

So, Peter worked with Paul, and at length they went to Rome. Their collaboration was not without its disagreements, but the success they enjoyed in constructing their Church served to bind them together.

I would like to add this. It is said that one day on the outskirts of Rome, near the end of his life, Peter saw Christ appear before him, his expression grave and pained. 'Master, where are you going?' asked Peter, and Jesus replied 'To Rome.' Peter asked him why, and our Lord answered, 'Why need you ask? To be crucified anew.'

According to our Christians, Simon Peter was shocked by this. They say he feared, as the Bishop of Rome, that he might have neglected his flock. I view the matter in another way. I like to think that Peter saw, in a moment of vision, his betrayal of truth. I like to think of this man who had once been my friend, that when he asked to be placed upside down on the cross on which, in the reign of that monster, Nero, they were going to kill him, he meant this as a sign. He had seen his error, and was filled with remorse.

I like to think that Peter, on that cross in Rome, had complete humility at last.

PAUL'S GOSPEL

What seems to me strange, though, is the way that people say Christ's wisdom and the reasonings of Paul are just the same—or that Paul too had our Lord's capacity for teaching, or that Paul, who everywhere bound his converts in the chains of mental slavery, was 'the free Spirit's apostle'. These things I cannot understand.

What did Paul of Tarsus have to do with Jesus Christ? He never met him. Nor do I believe he saw him in a vision. What I think took place upon that hot road to Damascus is that he saw, or saw and heard, his own self-doubt projected. But he did not see Jesus Christ—no, neither then nor later. What he saw was light, which is common among the ambitious. And thereafter, whatever befell him, he considered it miraculous—because he was Paul, the chosen one.

Yet not once, in all his writings, does he speak about the Jesus who had lived among us like an elder brother. Not even once does he show any interest in him. Nor does he quote him directly or allude to his sayings, though now and then he takes the words of Jesus and claims them for his own—as in that chapter on love with which he interrupts his letter to the church in Corinth. Word for word, this is what Christ said to the Essenes.

As to those who have convinced themselves that Paul and Jesus shared one mind, they must picture Christ as a philosopher, rehearsing theories of the Ancients while adding here and there some speculation of his own. But Jesus was the Son of God. He was divine. His teachings were absolute, true and spontaneous. He did not have to think them out, debate them with himself and then revise them, in the manner of philosophers. He learned them in no school, derived them from no teacher, and read them in no book—since, from the very first, the Gospel was his own.

Paul, by contrast, speculates and argues, he uses terms that Jesus never used, his words go round and round, he contradicts himself, he piles thought upon thought and constructs a system which does not make any sense—and our Christians call this nonsense 'transcendental'.

In this system of Paul's we discover, not the understanding of wrongdoing, of suffering and resurrection, which Jesus sought to give us, but just its opposite.

For Paul, the flesh is sinful in itself. 'For I know that nothing good dwells within me, that is, within my flesh,' he says, speaking of 'the law of sin which dwells within my members.' But if the flesh is sinful, then what of the world itself? What of matter? By extension, these must also be evil. But if the world is essentially sinful, then what of the God who created it?

We are close to the conjectures of the Gnostics with their *Demiurge* here, except that they are led by their beliefs into a kind of anarchy, whereas Paul extols authority.

But God is goodness itself, and would hardly have created such a sinful world, nor would he have let any 'demiurge' make such a world. For let us recall how Jesus spoke of God: as his holy, benevolent Father.

So, a good God would not have made all men to blame through Adam, or have implanted sinfulness in flesh and matter. These things are innocent. It is what men do with flesh and matter that is or is not sinful. I remember Jesus saying this after the resurrection. Peter inquired of him, 'Lord, what is the sin of the world?' and he replied: 'The world has no sin as you mean it, but it is men who manufacture sin when they commit things like adultery, or hand themselves over to anger or fear.'

Not that Paul draws all his thoughts to their conclusion, but still: this theory that the world was made of evil by an evil god is implicit in what he says. His god is a wrathful one, the storms of judgement itch in his hands.

And the Son, in this gospel of Paul's, is little more than a cypher, an abstraction. His words count for nothing, the life he lived amongst us is of no significance and his resurrection in the body is immaterial, as far as Paul is concerned—but his death: his death on the cross is what matters. For by this, the wrathful god of law and judgement is believed to have exempted those within Paul's Church from sin.

No, it does not make sense . . . but it is enough for Paul to build his Church upon, for he says to those he would convert: 'Christ died for your sins, therefore you owe him your faith . . . and if you do not have faith in him, you will be guilty forever.' In short, a kind of belief is extorted from seekers.

This matter of exemption from sin, however: what is it and what does it mean? For according to Paul, when we believe in Christ Jesus we are no longer under law but under grace . . . yet what does this grace give us? And what has become of the law? In practice, in both cases: nothing. We are allegedly under grace, but still we must not sin, we must not 'yield our members to sin as instruments of wickedness'; we must go on as before. We are under grace, but 'the law is holy still' and we are not to deny it—unless it be to eat with Gentiles.

So what have we gained? In actual fact, and in the present: nothing. But we can look forward at last to eternal life, at the time of judgement. And why? Why should we be so blessed? Because we believe in Christ Jesus. Our faith has justified us.

I am asked what is meant by this *justification*, and I reply: I do not know. If it means that solely through our belief in Jesus we are saved, then I say that the devil himself will go first to the Kingdom of Heaven, for, if anyone does, he must believe in Christ's reality.

After all, belief is easy. A man like Caiaphas believed in God, yet what came out of that belief? The persecution of Christ. The Pharisees who tried their best to trap Lord Jesus in their snares of doctrine had belief in God, yet it was nothing but a God made in the image of themselves. The philosophers who split hairs with Christ would sometimes say, 'We grant you, God exists,' yet who were they to favour God with their belief? Even now in our churches I hear many say, 'Oh, for my part, I believe that God is such and such' or 'I believe that God is so and so' . . . when God is far beyond their small conceptions and conceits.

Such belief is mere conditioning. It constitutes *opinion* and ventures nowhere near the state of *faith*. And God is no more circumscribed by such belief than he is by thought or feeling.

He can only be known by those who know their Spirit.

And so I do not give two pennies for this 'faith' of which Paul speaks, and by which he believes he is 'justified'. We believed in Jesus and saw his miracles, and yet he told us that we had no faith, saying: 'If you have faith as a grain of mustard seed, you will say to this mountain, "Move hence to yonder place," and it will move; and nothing will be impossible to you.' Therefore, faith that is true is profound. It can be called a dimension of *gnosis*. It is knowledge's power—where by 'knowledge' is meant the immediate awareness of truth, or the Spirit, or God.

Faith is something rare. To see to its growth is a lifetime's work. And because of the fact that it *knows*, it need neither threaten nor preach, it need not show off, it need not impose itself on others in order to sustain itself. Because it is something that *knows* the Divine, it does not set limits to God, does not seek to restrict him to one Incarnation in one place at one time, or to one or two texts at the most. Because it knows and is at one with the Divine, it cannot have anxiety; it has serenity and certainty; there comes from it the light of love.

But for Paul, his 'faith' was something that excused his former sins, his persecution of our brethren in the time before his journey to Damascus; his malice and his pride. He could never accept his own criminality, and thus asserted that, before they believe in our Lord, *all* men are bound to sin, being under law—while after believing, they are all of them justified, being under grace. According to this scheme of things, Paul himself was blameless: for at first he could not help but sin—or, if you like, he could not help it that the sin within him sinned. And later, once converted, he could not sin however much he might have wished to, since he was under grace.

Yet after being baptised by Paul and in spite of being under grace, his disciples still indulged in what the world calls *sin*. So, how was Paul's philosophy to cope with this? How could it explain away their immorality? It could not. At the same time, the indiscretions of his followers could not be allowed free rein, or they would have made a mockery of Paul's gospel. Therefore, he introduced a cold, dry piety into the Church, with fearful penalties for those found guilty of unrighteousness. And who was their judge? Why—Paul, of course. Not that he cared for the judgement of others upon himself, declaring that with him it was 'a very small thing that

I should be judged by you or by any human court. I do not even judge myself. I am not aware of anything against myself, but I am not thereby acquitted. It is the Lord who judges me.' Not so, however, with those over whom he presided. Not so with the ones he found guilty! They were sentenced to be 'given to Satan that their flesh might be destroyed'. And as for those who questioned his commands, they were not to be recognised; while those who disputed his gospel were pronounced accursed.

How was it that Paul could live by one law, while saying to his disciples: 'You must live by another'? Because—in his own words—he believed himself to be the master-builder of the Church, and the others but day labourers. Or, again, he called himself their father: that is, one whose word was law. Or he felt himself to be Christ's chosen go-between—hence, he decreed that his converts should: 'imitate me, as I imitate Christ'.

Yet by mimicking Paul, what did they hope to achieve? They could become possessed, perhaps: they could start to babble in tongues, or laugh uncontrollably, or mutter senseless prophecies; and perhaps the lonely could experience the sympathy of others, and those who wanted something to believe in could acquire it—but no one could in truth be born again, however much they stated: 'We are born again! We are born again!' for Paul denied the Mother. He discounted that power of hers through which such birth takes place.

Paul tried to claim that his Church and the Kingdom of Heaven were one and the same, or, worse, he tried to substitute the former for the latter.

So, nothing *real* could come of Paul's religion, for there was no substance to it. Yet I think that he sensed this emptiness, and therefore impressed upon his followers the need to think, not of the present, but of the time to come. Thus, many have claimed that they long for their deaths, when the Kingdom of God will be opened to them—and they confess they only live begrudgingly, or so that they can worship God while in the flesh. Thus, truth is cast into the future, and from this world to another, although our Lord said plainly that: 'My Father's Kingdom is spread out upon the Earth, yet men do not perceive it.'

Hence, the gospel of Paul is a dull, conditioned waiting for the end, when his abstract Christ will wreak his vengeance on all sinners, or, in other words, on those outside the Church, and will call up the ones who believe to a magical world in the clouds.

HUMILITY

And while Paul's disciples wait, the ruling powers hold sway. Yet Paul does not argue with this. 'Let all who are slaves regard their masters as deserving of all honour,' says Paul to Timothy; 'Let everyone be subject to the governing authorities. For there is no authority except from God, and those that exist have been made by God. Therefore he who resists the authorities resists what God has appointed, and those who resist will incur a judgement,' he declares to the Romans, in spite of the evil of slavery and in spite of corrupt and tyrannical rulers. Consider Herod, who was in authority, and who massacred the innocents. Or consider his successor, Herod Antipas, who beheaded John the Baptist. Or consider Pilate, who washed his hands of his guilt, yet still let Christ be scourged and crucified.

Now, it is true that Jesus praised the peacemakers, that he suffered himself to be executed, that he blessed the meek. It is true, as well, that he said that we should: 'Render unto Caesar what is Caesar's'—yet at the same time he flouted the power of the Pharisees and denounced all oppression of man by man. He did not want us to be arrogant, but neither did he want us to bow down before the arrogance of others.

And who are the possessed, but those who have accepted someone else's domination? Who else were the ones to whom he said that they should leave their mothers and their fathers if they were to follow him, but the seekers who lived in subjection to the past, overburdened with attachments, sympathies and habits? For, while oppressors are unwelcome in God's Kingdom, so also are the slavish.

Paul, in contrast, preached complete acceptance of the powers that be. This might have been because he was himself a Roman citizen and took the Roman point of view; or, just as likely, it was because he wished his own authority to go unchallenged—and the same with the bishops and priests, archdeacons and deacons he was busy appointing. He did not want to cultivate rebellion in daily life, in case it found its way into his Church.

Jesus said that whosoever humbles himself will be exalted, but with Paul there is an exaltation of authority. And while the Kingdom of Heaven that Jesus described is a place for the children of joy, for Paul it is ruled by a god surrounded by his ministers of state in all their hierarchy and pomp, with lesser officers employed to keep the innocent away.

SUFFERING

Now, to the question of *suffering*. Paul enumerates his sufferings with pride, he boasts of his anxieties, of how he was endangered in the wilderness, of how he was shipwrecked and beaten with rods. He declares he has great sorrow and unceasing anguish in his heart, and he speaks of the thorn in his flesh that cannot be healed.

He boasts of these things because he wants them to be taken as a mark of his authority. It is as though he says: 'How greatly I have suffered—therefore the work I have done for Christ must be great as well.' Likewise, he proclaims that: 'I am the least of the apostles,' yet he would have us believe that in truth he is the greatest, for 'I worked harder than any of them.' His weakness he makes into the badge of his apostleship, and his sickness he refigures as a sign of his perfection, maintaining that the Lord assured him: 'my grace is sufficient for you, for my power is made perfect in weakness.'

Thus common sense is turned upon its head. The disorders that afflict a man are declared to be his strengths—when that man is Paul.

But there is something more in this, for Paul would have it that his sufferings are part of Christ's sufferings, or even that he himself made up, in his trials, for what our Lord omitted. And so he tells the Colossians, 'I rejoice in my sufferings for your sake, and in my flesh complete what is lacking in Christ's afflictions for the sake of his body, that is, the Church.' Not that Jesus considered his body to be the Church, for that is Paul's doctrine. But this is remarkable, for it betrays what Paul believed: that he himself had taken on Christ's mantle, was now wearing his crown. I think this was written in Paul's latter days, in Rome.

To suffer is good, says Paul. Whatever we suffer as Christians, it is for Jesus's sake, he tells the Philippians—and also, perhaps, it is so that we may become like Christ. Indeed, he asserts that 'for his sake I have suffered the loss of all things,' but this does not matter, since it has been in order that: 'I may share his sufferings, becoming like him in his death, that if possible I may attain the resurrection from the dead.'

The circle, then, is closed. In the gospel preached by Paul, only a fantastic grace is offered, a hypothetical freedom accorded. No one is changed in actuality—and thus their sufferings continue. But far from drawing from this the conclusion that nothing has really happened, Paul turns it to his advantage. His converts must still suffer, yes—but that is good, because it is a symbol of their holiness, it contributes to Christ's own glory, it adds to all the Lord for his part suffered, and it completes what he neglected.

This is nothing but a mockery of what Lord Jesus did. He suffered—insofar as he could suffer—so that we, his younger brothers, would not have to suffer. When he crucified himself he took our sins upon him, which is to say that he enabled us to free ourselves, if we so desire, from the momentum of the deeds done in our past. Whenever those deeds are bad or whenever we attach ourselves to them, that momentum accrues in our life to the point where it brings about our suffering, and so it goes on from life to life—but Jesus freed us from this cycle of involvement and reaction.

Jesus freed us, if we wish to be free, by being crucified. He freed us by opening the *Agnya Chakra* within us through his crucifixion. He opened up the gateway to the Kingdom. He made it easy to enter the present, from which the moods of pain and sorrow that must always come can be observed by us without our being part of them. Indeed, we can witness things joyfully, for the mood of the Spirit is joy. The mood of truth is joy.

And that is why it is a sin to bask in suffering, and why this homage paid to suffering is perverse. Jesus came to make men happy, and those who longed for enduring delight gathered round him. Their illnesses he healed and their confusion he dispelled, and wherever there was darkness he brought light-heartedness and light. He did not say: 'My burden is heavy,' no, he said: 'My burden is light.' But those who seek the world and turn their backs on Christ will have to bear the world's weight on their shoulders, and those who wish for suffering will find it.

He sang the song of everlasting joy, and those who longed for such joy were enraptured.

THE SUMMONS

In the end, we required Paul to come to Jerusalem, that he might explain himself. In his own words, he came 'by revelation'—not that that was the case at all. James commanded Paul to come before the year was out, for during all this time he had shunned Judea, and as many as fourteen years had passed since we had last set eyes on him.

He finally arrived with two of his disciples: the one named Titus, the other, Barnabus. He asked what it was that we wanted of him—a show of meekness which took James off guard. He said we wished to know what Paul was teaching.

Very well, he would tell us—and so he did, but in so complex, evasive and rambling a way that I think we were all bemused. Here and there we said, 'This is too much,' or 'This is too little,' and each time he gave way, and gave way—but I felt that these were superficialities when what was at fault was the essence.

In those days, though, I did not see things clearly. And although we knew those words of Jesus: 'Many will call me as though they know me, but I will not know them,' we could not yet apply them to a man who, it seemed, had laboured so hard in Christ's name.

Besides which, Paul had clothed himself in the whole armour of the small self, and his nature was a mystery to us. Moreover, the dead spirits he had gathered about him affected us: we felt oppressed: they dulled the processes of thought.

Of his work in constructing the Church, he was modest in his claims. 'But if I have erred in building up the Church of Christ our Lord, then I ask you to correct me,' he concluded, and he saw, as I saw, that James was at a loss.

Still, he made a few recommendations. He exhorted Paul to speak more of Jesus the Son of Man, to relay Christ's teachings of the Kingdom, to care for the poor and oppressed (whom Paul had neglected, since the poor do not fund churches), and to give up his speaking in tongues. James stressed the need for brotherhood among the followers of Christ and the value of the heart in all we said, and thought, and did. And to our surprise he met with no resistance. Paul acceded to each request, except in the matter of speaking in tongues. He could do nothing about it, he said, for the gifts of the Lord were the Lord's alone to give or take away.

Then, he announced his departure—and as suddenly as he had come, he left.

It was not long before we heard more news of Paul, however. Not by one iota had he changed his gospel: he still prophesied in tongues, still put an abstract, impersonal Christ in place of the Son of Man, still based his religion on power, not on love, and still laid curses on his enemies.

Seeing how far things had gone, we decided we must act. Paul's work had at last to be countered. But how were we to do this? For Paul had entered the field of seeking and sown his tares among the wheat, and we could not simply root them out without the wheat's loss also. No more than we could say that all he taught was true could we proclaim that all he taught was false; yet in those days men and women wanted certainties, not ambiguities, complexities and fine distinctions. They did not want to sift through dust and stones for gold, they wanted gold already fashioned.

And so, our task was difficult. We sent letters, we sent messengers. It was the latter whom Paul called spies, and the former to which he responded when he wrote epistles to the Galatians and Corinthians. And his anger towards us shows through, when he speaks of 'those who were reputed to be something (what they were makes no difference to me; God shows no partiality)' and of 'James and John and Cephas (for this was after he had clashed with Peter, in Antioch), who were reputed to be pillars.' He betrays his agitation at our letters when he states: 'I think I am not in the least inferior to these superlative apostles,' and again, 'for I am not at all inferior to these superlative apostles, even though I am nothing.'

As we now found to our cost, Paul had formed his Church in such a way that it could not be disestablished in a few days or a year. Meanwhile, there were troubles in Judea of another kind, and Jerusalem was destroyed. Our little fellowship was broken up. Thomas had taken fright already at the course the Church was following, and after rejoining us briefly had soon returned to India; now other believers gave way to doubts, notwithstanding the fact that Jesus had foretold this calamity. The letters we had written to Paul were lost. In a word, our work was interrupted—while his was done.

PAUL: IN CONCLUSION

At last Paul died in Rome, yet his passing brought us no relief. Whereas we had tried to build free men, he had built a structure to enclose them: orthodox, hierarchical, inflexible and narrow—and not least, I fear, enduring. We shall die, but his Church will outlive us all: and Paul's kind will still trouble the children of light with their nets of dark shadow, at least until the advent of the Comforter.

Sometimes, here in Ephesus, our Christians take my arguments for ravings, my caveats for dreams. They ask if, in their Church, they do not worship God the Father, and try as best they can to follow the commandments, and seek to love each other, just as Paul advised. And I reply, 'Yes, and these things are far from insignificant.' All the same, I know what Paul's disciples would have done to Thomas, had they been able to get hold of him, and I know very well what they would do to me if they could read this book of memories.

'And although Paul talked of Christ, and of morality, these things are only half the story,' I go on. 'Having heard fragments, you say, "This much is good, therefore all the story must be good," but you do not see who is telling the story, nor how he tells it.'

Both Jesus and Paul spoke of truth, but the one was divine and his speech expressed that quality: he *was* the truth, and whatever he uttered was truth; while the other was a man of strong antipathies, with blood on his hands and a compelling need to dominate—and his speech too expressed his quality: for as the man is in his inner nature, so will be the value of his words.

Jesus spoke of truth as one who holds a torch to light the darkness; he holds it still and men are drawn to it—and if they wish, they may light their own lamps from it; whereas Paul spoke of truth with arguments and rhetoric, cajoling men by playing on their hopes and fears, employing threats, inventing regulations. He claimed to be the bearer of the light of truth, but whatever sparks of truth were in his subject to begin with, they vanished when he preached—just as when a lamp is flourished in the air too violently, its light will waver and go out.

To those who exonerate Paul, I say again: 'You do not understand his character, nor do you notice how he takes the word of Christ and reinterprets it: you do not see what elements have been imported and what omitted, how the ending has been changed and the meaning turned about.' For Jesus taught the Gospel of eternal life, but in the Church of Paul of Tarsus a creed of death is preached.

I see this and am filled with disquiet. I see the pilgrim searching for God's Kingdom, and I see his many trials. I see him lost in the desert, when suddenly he meets a group of travellers. They seem to be friendly, and they tell him they know of the country of which he dreams. Indeed, they have travelled from there, they say—they have come looking for seekers like him—and to that innocent, beautiful land they are just now returning. They speak of Jesus Christ, the Saviour, and, enthralled, he follows them. But time goes by, and still they do not reach the Kingdom. The travellers, who have introduced themselves as Christians, conduct mock-rituals, and put on airs and graces, and threaten those who question them—but all the while they move in circles. Then the pilgrim understands: they are not enlightened souls at all but robbers, and he is being led not into freedom, but captivity.

I know that when I speak like this, men are affronted. They may have no regard for Paul, yet they complain, 'Why be so hard on him, too hard? You preach compassion, but where is your compassion now?'

I reply: 'The tolerance of negativity is not compassion.'

Again they say, 'Yet why speak so much and so harshly of Paul, when it was Caiaphas who persecuted Christ, it was Judas who betrayed him, it was Pilate who let him be killed?'

I answer: 'A man comes somewhere where the people are enslaved. His sole wish is to free them and, indeed, he is their rightful king—yet a number of men oppose him.

'Now which of these men, do you think, will cause that king most pain? Those who openly declare themselves to be his enemies? Or else those self-appointed friends who claim to act on his behalf, while corrupting both his image and his work?

'It is latter, surely, who create the greatest harm, and amongst us their leader was Paul.'

I do not think he knew who Jesus was. What he knew, believed in, fought for, and built his Church upon was merely an *idea*, not truth.

And now I see him as he was. At first I took him for an evil man, bent upon our destruction. Then he believed himself converted, and, mistrusting the thoughts of my heart—and for fear of being branded unforgiving—I half-believed him altered too. Then I felt: he is a little overzealous, nothing more. Still later, I considered him mistaken and in dire need of correction. But now I see that Paul of Tarsus was destructive all along. When he fell on the road to Damascus he changed his mind the way a man puts on a different outer garment, but in his essence stays the same. While renouncing Pharisaism, he still retained his small, ambitious self, and in the image of that self he made his Church.

To sum up the matter in plain words: he was a devil out and out.

DETACHMENT

Jesus came to make men happy. And that was here in this world: in this world of which he was the essence.

It is true that he had overcome the world—or, rather, he was from first to last beyond the world—yet he did not therefore disdain this world. No more was he blind to its beauty than he was deaf to the cries of the ones lost within it.

Under the cedars of Lebanon outside Tiberias, a rose in his hands, I seem to see him now—not turning his back on the world or looking down with hooded eyes, as some men suppose he behaved—but bestowing grace on this abundant earth and enjoying it, and wishing us to enjoy it too.

Yet he was not in any way involved in the world, and he wished us to express that same detachment also. He said: 'Become as passers-by,' and again, 'This world is a bridge. Pass over it, but do not build your house upon it.' By which he meant: 'Enjoy this world, somewhat as passers-by enjoy the scenery they move through on their way from one place to another.' Not being natives of the place, they feel no attachment to the mountains and valleys through which their journey takes them, nor to the people they meet; and because they are not attached, they can enjoy what they behold: this moon of silica, which they can never touch, or sea of jade, or sea, at dusk, of lapis lazuli which they can never own, or the grandeur of the starry night, which they can never possess, or the patterns on the foreign coins which are of no use to them beyond the border, or the beauty of the dark-eyed girl who brings them sugared water in a wayside inn, or who runs ahead while laughing through the gateway of a saffron-coloured city which they will never see again.

He did not come to refuse or deny us the world, but to teach the art of joy. He called us from our homes, our parents, our past, from submission and ambition, and from the world as object of desire and satisfaction, dissatisfaction and desire—not to give us nothing in return, but just the opposite: to give us everything. To show us that, while we live here for a while, our homeland is eternity.

To show us we are the Spirit.

And when this is known as *gnosis*: as a part of our awareness: then we begin to see this world for what it is. We see it as if by a homeward-bound road we are leaving it, or as if we have just arrived; our heart goes out to it, and we look upon its citizens with unreserved compassion.

FIRE

Jesus came to make men happy. When he lived among us he did all he could to give us happiness.

Men brought him their anger, and in return he offered them the honey of his kindness. Women brought him their pain, and in return he offered them the balm of his intelligence.

Once we came to an inn where the host was an old, ill-tempered man who grumbled while he served us. When he had left the room, Jesus said: 'You see that man, how old he is, how close to death. And what has he distilled from the fullness of his years? Not the nectar of wisdom, but the sour wine of a sharp tongue and an unresponsive heart.' Andrew said: 'Yes, he is like a High Priest,' and Jesus laughed.

Then he said, 'The priests will tell you that God made Man in his own image, and it is true. But do they think that God is an old embittered man like themselves, whose chief pleasure is interdiction? No,' he said, 'He is not like that at all.'

Then he moved his hands so that one was held palm out towards us while the other was raised in blessing. His head was outlined against the window, through which were visible the winter stars, while above him, on the lintel, stood a round brass dish whose hammered, polished surface mirrored back the fire that burned inside that little room—and thus he was crowned both with starlight and flames. And he might have been referring to himself when he continued: 'God is a child who is older than time.'

THE DIAMOND

Jesus came to make men happy. He said: 'If you know your Spirit, you need never be unhappy—for the Spirit is joy, and when a man has become the Spirit he finds a joy in work as well as in play, a joy in giving as well as in receiving, joy even in the heart of sorrow and a joy in sacrifice. And when he comes to his death he finds joy and not grieving, and angels not mourning but dancing.'

'Are these joys all the same or are they different?' asked Bartholomew.

'They are the same and also different,' the Lord replied. 'You have seen a diamond, and you have seen how it is one stone in itself, yet catches the light in different ways and takes on different hues. As many as the moments in eternity are the numberless colours of joy, to those who know their Spirit.'

LIGHT-HEARTEDNESS

Jesus came to make men happy, and when, as sometimes happened, we felt weary or discouraged, he would remonstrate with us, saying: 'When a master frees his slaves, do you think they wear long faces and indulge in sorrow? No, they laugh and sing. But here the Son of Man is freeing you from a bondage more profound than any human slavery, so think of your blessings and be glad.'

And again he said: 'While the light shines, still the children play; therefore while the Light is with you, enjoy the play of the Light upon you.

'And if you become the Light, you will enjoy that play forever.'

But Paul and his kind outlaw light-heartedness. 'Let there be no levity,' he states in his letters, when speaking of his Church, and 'Deacons and women must be serious,' and so forth.

And what of children? What of the little ones whom Jesus loved? I do not think there can be a place for them where such a solemn piety prevails, either in the churches Paul established or in the Catacombs of Rome, among the bones of the dead.

DARKNESS

And now our priests have taken to wearing black, as though they have come to mourn, not celebrate, and I hear them intone the prayers in slow and cultivated voices, as though speaking of death to the dead; and it would not surprise me if, one day, they take an emblem of death for their badge of office, the sign of their authority.

Then they will wear around their necks the cross of crucifixion, and not in their eyes the light of resurrection.

And in Rome: the way they gather and eat in what has become a graveyard: as though it is fitting to worship the Lord of Life in a place of death.

I know: they use those catacombs for fear of persecution. But Jesus said to leave the dead behind—not to bring them with us, as these men do.

Because of their superstition, or because of a meaningless sentimentality, they have brought the relics of the dead into their temples, and this custom, once established, is being reproduced wherever men love Christ. But what is now dead cannot succour the living, nor is its fleshly husk of value to the soul that seeks another dwelling-place, another life.

So, let us give to the fire what belongs to the past, with due formality, and attend to the present, where truth abides.

Besides which, dead things, dead ideas and dead proclivities can lure the unappeased, frustrated souls who have not released their grip upon this world. Interfering or malevolent, these ghosts exist as parasites upon the living, and if in our habits and our places of worship we continue to cling to the dead, the dead will in turn cling to us.

And to those who declare: 'These are fictions of John's, again he overstates the case,' I reply that those who are bring the dead into the house of Christ are bringing death into the temple of the human being; while those who clothe themselves in darkness in the name of holiness, those who dwell upon the stations of the cross in their pursuit of liberation, those who take upon themselves a power to which they have no right: to bless, baptise, and pardon sins, and excommunicate; and those who dominate, or spread oppression, in the holy name of Jesus: these ones bring darkness to the human heart.

THE INCARNATIONS

Once, a traveller from Greece referred to Socrates of Athens, and Jesus said: 'I know him,' as if that wise philosopher were still alive and standing next to him, also facing the crowd, also saying alongside our Lord: 'Seek the Spirit within you,' and not in his grave these five hundred years.

Then another man, an Indian, asked: 'What of the Buddha?' At which a merchant added: 'And what of Mahavira of the Jains?' And again our Lord half-smiled to his right and left, as though to brother princes in a court we could not see. Then he spoke, not only to those travellers but to everyone assembled there, saying: 'Those not against me are with me. The Buddha stands to one side of the Son, and Mahavira to the other. And Socrates, the teacher, was of God, as was Zoroaster and the others. Those not against me are with me.'

That is what he said in the public square in Jerusalem. But Paul later changed this to: 'Those not with me are against me.' He wanted it to seem that only those who follow Christ by name, who are baptised by priests and who belong to the Church, may enter the Kingdom of God—for he thought in terms of power and exclusivity, and not of integration, love, and common sense.

GNOSIS

I thought: I shall establish another tradition, a different kind of Christianity. In this, I shall emphasise *gnosis*. I shall argue that we do not follow Christ by forming an organisation and joining that organisation, by learning by rote the texts of Christianity, by binding ourselves to rules or observing rituals. Nor do we follow him by stressing self-denial. He did not ask us to withdraw into the mountains; he never told us to subdue the flesh, or the mind, or desire, through the practice of mortification. He did not say: 'Go, hunt the golden mean at the extremities,' or: 'Go, search for joy in pain.' Nor are his Father and his Mother pleased when we act out his agony in celebration.

How, then, can we serve him? We please him by seeking the Spirit, and we follow him best by *becoming* that Spirit. For the latter is peace and compassion, it is joy and completion. It is wisdom and knowledge, it is faith, it is love. Therefore, he who is the Spirit in reality is possessed of all these qualities. He is peaceful, and faithful, and wise. He has recovered innocence. He knows how far to go and where to stop or turn aside. In short, the one who is the Spirit is a Christian.

Thus, I wanted to speak about *knowing* the Spirit, and since many agreed that this was the aim of our search, they took the name: 'Knowers', or *Gnostics*.

But this teaching was displeasing to Paul's followers—and so, as far as they were able to, they outlawed and suppressed it. In reaction, many malcontents and rebels allied themselves with this new Gnostic faith, bringing with them notions that bore no relation to Christ's work and pretending to a knowledge of the Spirit that was not yet theirs to claim. And now, if I venture among them, I hear only talk about gnosis among them, only whispers and rumours of truth. The water of life is referred to in full, but they offer me none to drink. Nor do I see the truth embodied in their lives, but only waywardness in their pursuit of truth—some moving to the right side, into intellectual fantasy or self-denial, and some towards the left, to sensual abandonment.

A disenchantment with the world unites them, it being their conviction that Almighty God could not have made this Earth: it is too sick with evil, too rife with sin.

For them the world has come about through error; it is innately contradictory, and the work not of Almighty God but of a mediating deity, a demiurge whom some call *Jaldabaoth*: a powerful, self-seeking entity inimical to Man.

Although they believe in the Spirit, they think of it as having been imprisoned inside matter, which they take to be evil; and the way in which the planets, through their movements, indicate our human character is interpreted by them as our enslavement by the archons.

I see the same conditions: how the Spirit is hidden in men and women, how our characters are limited, how matter distracts us, and so forth; but I differ in my conclusions. To these present-day Gnostics the Creation is a useless thing, it is imposed upon the Spirit, it has to be dispensed with; but in the cypress trees at dusk, or in the gold light on the hills, or in the crocuses of Nazareth, or in music or a child's eyes, I find it the case even now—or especially now, when so soon I must leave it—that matter can communicate the Spirit.

In short, their demiurge I do not recognise. Their abstruse and contradictory cosmogonies, by which they try to reason out the origin and purpose of this world, I find ridiculous. And their interpretation of Sophia as being first in error, and then divided into two: a greater and a lesser: I find absurd.

Here and there a saying of Jesus is reported in their gospels, but only as a source for esoteric speculation; while words are put into the mouths of the apostles with no regard for what was really said; and all in all a mystique is created, by which the seeker is persuaded that these Gnostics are possessed of secret wisdom.

But wisdom lies in what is simple, not in what is strange and convoluted. Wisdom is straightforward, innocent and childlike, like Lord Jesus Christ himself, not labyrinthine and occult. And insofar as they reject the paths that children tread, these so-called Gnostics have entirely lost their way . . .

THE MOTHER AND CHILD

Some proclaim that they worship the Goddess, yet they cannot accept the Son. Others worship the Son, yet disregard the Mother.

Now, Jesus said that all our sins can be forgiven except the sin against the Holy Ghost. But Mary said in after days that no, this is not so. The sin against the Holy Ghost, herself, may be forgiven—but not the sin against the Son.

For the Son is the door, and if we turn away from it, or slam it shut with our perversions or our anger, conditioning or selfishness—then the Kingdom must be closed to us.

So: the Mother and Son both act as one. Out of love, the former wants to please the latter, and out of love the latter wants to please the former; and though their roles are different, still in their work they are concerted and united, there is no argument between them. Therefore those who try to pit the one against the other, or neglect the one in favour of the other, are very much in error.

And when the Mother comes back as the Comforter, the Son will be with her to protect and assist her, saying, 'This one is truly a seeker; he deserves his redemption, so let him be enlightened,' or: 'That one is not a true seeker; his time has not come, let him be.' For: 'I am my Mother's power personified,' said Jesus Christ, 'and if I say, "Yes," then it will be yes, while if I say, "No", then it will be no.'

I would add that when, in my heart, in truth, I praise the Son—then I feel the Mother's pleasure like the breath of angels on my head and hands. But when I praise the Mother, the Comforter, directly—when in my heart, in truth, I praise her—then it is as though the Son himself blows down her sweet and cooling, blissful wind of love upon me and within me.

PATMOS

In the reign of Domitian I was summoned to Rome and tortured. And there I witnessed darkness in the shape of men, there I saw King Death in the ascendant, the satanic spectre fully formed.

The things that happened there were difficult to comprehend: for were we not believers in the living God? Yet time after time those devils used us for their sport.

I prayed. I sought comfort in understanding. But it was easy to begin to believe, as many of us now believed, that, after all, the world was evil. That it was ruled by demonic powers and could not be transformed but had to be destroyed.

I did not believe this. And yet the weight of such an argument impressed me. I had hoped to live to see a world of light; instead the innocents were massacred anew. I had wished to see our Lord acknowledged everywhere, but no, it was the demons who exacted homage, who described themselves as gods and had men worship them. So, when confronted with the evil of a Nero or Tigellinus, it was no wonder that our comrades hardened their resolve against the world.

I thought: I too shall steel myself against this fleeting earthly life, but when I looked inside myself I found my heart was hard already.

Later, once banished to Patmos, I repented of my mistakes, my failures, my turning too much towards the world, and I sought to give myself to righteousness entirely. I laboured hard, became reclusive, strove with myself, spent hours each day in contemplation and self-discipline.

If the pathway to the Kingdom were a spiral stairway, then in making my ascent by trying to perfect myself, I was adhering to the central pillar. But that is where the steps are narrowest, and increasingly my climb seemed arduous and dangerous. As once before, I lived in fear of falling.

This added to the tension in my soul.

Moreover, it was bitter to be placed in exile, it was bitter to be thrown out to the margin of the world. I wished to spread Christ's gospel, but I was living like a useless thing in isolation. And all the while, the progress of our Church disturbed me.

Not that that progress was slow—on the contrary, it was growing ever faster; but even had our numbers been depleted, or had they dwindled to a handful, I could have stood it better than to see what I was seeing clearly now: the making of a Church in which the Feminine was slighted and the Holy Ghost excluded, a Church in which submission to authority was put in place of being born anew, a Church infested with dead souls.

The story was an old one. What had been supposed to mediate the truth had itself assumed the name and powers of truth.

I saw this with such clarity, yet in my exile I was powerless. I saw that Paul had done his work efficiently—yet in the end, perhaps, it was succeeding through the force, in men and women, of their conditioning, and through their fondness for the small, blind, partial self. To set us free from their dominion was one reason why Christ came, yet while we granted him his triumph over all the rest: the devil, the world, the heart and the soul—and even our former conditioning—we could not yet abandon the *It is, it must be* of conditioning itself, nor could we be released from our *I am*. Thus, we redefined his meaning in the light of those attachments.

How else was it that we could say: when he speaks of love, the words of Jesus are eternal, but in denouncing the Scribes and Pharisees, his words belonged to one time only, a time now long since passed?

For the Pharisees and Scribes, the Sadducees and Zealots are found in all religions, under other names: they are types of men, varieties in which an adamant conditioning and small *I am* express themselves.

Of course, there are many servants of our Church who mean well and are sincere and kind. But their duty is neither to a Church made by the mind of Man nor to a God composed of thoughts and superstitions, but to the truth and the seekers of truth.

So, I watched from afar as my brothers and sisters constructed an illusory holy kingdom; I watched from afar, now bitterly and now in intellectual fury—and yet I could not help but be a member of that Church, since others said: 'Look, there is John the dreamer, a founder of our Church.'

And I recalled that while our Lord had enemies on every side, it was a friend who had betrayed him. Yes: with a kiss he was betrayed, by one who called himself a follower he was exchanged for silver, by one who claimed to represent him he was delivered up to Caiaphas, to Pilate, and to death. I remembered this, and felt at a loss, uncertain what to do.

It was in the course of these reflections that I imagined the Apocalypse.

BEAUTY

Now, all my life I had loved beauty, had followed beauty with my eyes and ears and mind.

Even as a child, the image of the New Jerusalem, the city of brotherly love, was beautiful to me; I saw its pattern displayed in my heart. In youth the flowers of Galilee were beautiful to me; on evenings when the air was scented with their fragrance I would sense the infinite involved within the finite, mysteriously, and the certainty of God's existence, his bewildering presence, would fill my being. In the face of a girl of Bethsaida I witnessed beauty's face: in her I saw infinity compressed, or so it seemed to me then, and infinity smiled. I heard beauty in music; in the music of harps and drums, in the hills dissolving in the evening, and in the waters of Tiberias I perceived eternity take sensuous form: although this happened only rarely, for what I mean by this feeling for beauty is the meeting of beholder and beheld in innocence.

Then, later, I perceived a subtle beauty in Christ's life: in the symbols that he gave us, in the art of his gestures, in the fire of his speech. When Jesus smiled—it might have been while watching children playing in the dusty streets of Nazareth . . . or once, I recall, inside his father's workshop, when taking up a piece of cedar wood, as yet unworked, and turning it this way and that in his hands as though considering, from an examination of its grain and weight, what he could make of it—then gazing intently at us, as though foretelling from the lines upon our faces, from the knots of our contradictions, from our dispositions and angularities, from our strengths and weaknesses, what he could yet make of us—and smiling—at such times I felt absolute beauty touch my heart.

But on Patmos my heart grew hard, and accordingly the sense of beauty left me. I searched for her in objects, I sought her in glamour of things, where she does not reside, and I did not find her.

Then in my bitterness I began to doubt that beauty has to do with truth, or that truth, which is pure, can be beautiful too.

So, I disavowed my love of beauty, believing it an impediment to righteousness. I turned my back upon the imagery around me, upon the summer stars and winter sea, the sunrise and the birds' songs and the daughters of the island, the sunset and the starry night: from now on all was one to me: a compound of unstable matter and futility.

But like a sleeping man who, though his eyes are shut to the world, cannot help but have dreams, so the poetry I had forsworn in outer life now reappeared within me in a different form, with violent power, refracted through my soul's imagination, in cataclysmic visions of events to come.

REVELATIONS

And in the seven lamp-stands the wise will see the seven *chakras*, and in the seven angels they will see the archetypes of God enthroned within the chakras. In the beasts and dragon they will see things gross and subtle, external and internal. In the mark of the beast they will see what only the enlightened can discern. In the dragon's pursuit of the woman they will see the dangers that the Comforter will face. And in the woman clothed with sunlight, crowned with stars, and with the moon beneath her feet, they will see the Comforter, the Counsellor, the Mother in her pure redeeming form, the Holy Ghost on Earth; while in the rider on the white horse they will see Lord Kalki, Jesus, the judge at the end of the Age, and his army of saints of shared intention, of a single compassionate heart.

AQUARIUS

In due course I was released from Patmos, and returned by sea to Ephesus. That same sea, that image of great fluid power contained, detached, and ever-moving, though also at rest within itself, had been my solace in the last days of my exile, and now my friends acquired a house for me near the harbour, that I might live within sight of the water, within sound of the gulls.

After every forceful effort one may suffer a reaction, and on concluding the *Revelations* I felt emptied of feeling and will. I felt close to the end of my life for which, at the same time, I knew I was not yet prepared.

In this manner things continued for some time.

Then, one day when the almond trees were in blossom, I was returning from the city to my house when, overcome with weariness and thirst, I sat down at the roadside to rest. A little while passed, and then around the corner, between the almond trees, came a woman holding on her head a water jar. Unhurriedly, with dignity, she walked, with her left hand swinging freely at her side, so to give her balance, and her right hand steadying the jar. She was poorly dressed—a water-seller, I supposed—and, like myself, the dust of the road was upon her. Perhaps she had found no buyers, for the highway was all but empty, and now she was returning to her hovel on the outskirts of the city. Meanwhile, a little boy, her son perhaps, came clapping his hands to a loose and graceful rhythm, half-walking, half-dancing from side to side in front of her. To the sheepskin belt around his waist an earthenware cup was tied, while as for his bearing and face, they were those of a young king in hiding, or else, perhaps, in exile. And so unhurriedly, evenly, steadily, did they advance towards me through the heat rising off the road and the shimmering, blossoming almond trees, that they might have been moving to the steps of a grave and stately dance, to the music of birds and cicadas and, far off, the sea. And I, an old man, observed them until I was no longer old, neither old nor young, and no longer thought of the wounds still paining me, the self-denial I had undergone to little purpose, my worries concerning the future.

At length they approached me, and with a grave and gentle expression the boy inquired if there were anything I wished for. My mouth was dry and speech was difficult.

'Some water, if you please,' I said.

Assenting, light-hearted, composed, he ran to his mother and held out the earthenware cup for her to fill with water, which, without a glance in my direction, she did. Then, just as swiftly, he returned, and with the laughter of the blackbird, singing, or with the laughter of the almond trees in the calm, Aegean wind, or with the laughter of one who belongs completely to the present, he waved aside the coin I offered and gave me what I had asked for, saying: 'This is for you.'

And I looked at his mother and saw in her eyes Sophia's eyes, the Mother's eyes, looking out of the eternal present back at me, the weary traveller, with undivided love.

She was looking at my Spirit, so it seemed, and I too was that Spirit looking back at her. I was looking through the gate of the eternal present where she stood, or we were both in that eternal present, each gazing at the other.

This was there, a little outside Ephesus, yet at the same time it was *here*, precisely here, in the numinous country of Heaven.

And I saw that this was where the Divine is to be found. But, as a rule, when we speak of Him or worship Him, we do so indirectly, in the form of a name, of a concept; and this is why men can say: 'I think such and such' or 'I believe so and so' about Almighty God; it is why they can organise religions and develop their theologies—or why they can deny Him, if they wish—because they do not know the Divine directly, they have not had that experience.

While everything outside that experience: the dusty road unwinding from one place to another; distant Ephesus, white in the white afternoon; the heat; that ageing body still belonging to a man named John—and our sufferings in Rome—those too: seemed finally unreal. Or these things comprised a play: a play of which the Spirit was the witness: a play which the imagination of the Holy Spirit bodies forth unceasingly; and the shape of that play became known to me, as though I were a child first discerning in the host of stars the outlines of the constellations.

A moment went by, and the boy and his mother passed on. I stood up, having drunk my fill, and continued on along the pathway home.

JUDGEMENT

Yet if it is a play, why should our lot be suffering? Why should it happen that, by taking after Christ, we should be met with persecution?

It is true: its cause is all the evil in the world. The evil hates the good and will attack it when it can. Nonetheless, one asks oneself the question: why, when we are Christians, can we not go safely through this life?

I believe that we are cared for, but that the power of God is not so active in the world as yet that we can be protected always. Besides which, we can make ourselves accessible to evil through our misbehaviour, and that is also why we suffer.

Such suffering is not the will of God, it is not God's desire, for God is love and is complete and thus has no particular desires; but when our actions take us to the left or right, they bring a reaction upon us, and that reaction is the fate which, as one or as many, we construct for ourselves.

Jesus came to open up the means within us to dissolve this fate, but if we still identify our small selves as the actors of our actions, if we continue acting and reacting, then again we bring about our fate, which again we must dissolve through disenchantment and forgiveness.

And the whole is a play, a drama. It is a play, though we who saw our comrades sacrificed to wild beasts in Rome, did not then see them in their subtle form rise up again, shake off the dust, and without a look behind fly into unimaginable light, and thence to other births, to other lives, the recurring combat with evil, the long eventful passage to Jerusalem.

And the play is not without direction. It is not that we are fated to go round and round, forever doing battle with the same satanic powers, forever erring, learning, seeking—for the shape of history is not a circle but is something like a spiral. As the seasons move, so we move in a recurring rhythm, but as the years pass by we move towards a judgement and a world transformed.

This I know in my heart.

Jesus said: 'I have cast a fire upon the world, and see, I am guarding it until it blazes.' As a purifying fire he came into the world, and because of that he said: 'They who are near to me are near the fire.' As a purifying fire he came into the world, because his mother's purifying fire was expressed in him—and so, whatever he could purify he purified, according to its receptivity. He was the active, outward form of her potential power. He was her power personified.

Yet men did not accept him, not as he was, so the fire was slow to spread. Only a few accepted him, and those who accepted the fire, the fire accepted. They became like fire, and the fire did not torment them, since fire does not burn fire. They became like fire because in them the Holy Spirit's fire was now awakened, and so the fire did not consume them: it did not burn what they were in reality, but only that which they were not. The fire consumed their needless habits and the small self's inessential matter, but it did not touch the Spirit: for the Spirit neither catches fire nor can it be extinguished.

They became like fire, or they are becoming like fire; it burns in their beings in moderation as they become the masters of the fire; ever more brightly it blazes within them, and they are as lamps in the darkness.

These are the saints who give light to the world.

But the saints are few and the fire is small. Jesus said: 'I came to cast a fire upon the Earth, and would it were kindled already!' because he was impatient for the judgement. Not that it was of interest to him to count our sins, to hold this or that against us, for a master does not pry into the business of his servants. But he wished to see his work fulfilled, he wished his devotees to see the New Jerusalem. He was anxious for the judgement not for judgement's sake, but that the Kingdom may be entered into, once the dross of evil and the trash of human pettiness are burned away. He was anxious for whatever is to be included in the Kingdom and not for what will be shut out: just as a sculptor is concerned not with the marble chips discarded but the figure taking shape beneath his chisel.

Still, his mother's patience was expressed in him, and so our Lord held back and waited—and still he waits, and waits, watching over the small fire of truth in this world.

But at the end of the Age, when the Holy Spirit appears, this purifying power will become a conflagration in the same way that a piece of wood, when kindled, only smoulders, but in time erupts in flame.

She will awaken this fire in all seekers of truth, and gradually, surprisingly, nation after nation will be set alight with this pure, metaphysical fire until the world's four quarters will become the furnaces of judgement.

Out of encompassing darkness the children of light will arise and cast off their small selves and everything dead within them: all will be burned: and they shall know the Spirit. But those who deny the Mother, and those who cling to their conditioning, and those who refuse to surrender their hold on the small, hard, delusory self, will themselves be at the mercy of the raging, lustral flames of mercy's holy fire, for what is unreal must at last be consumed.

And so, what to one man will be the fire of retribution will be to another what it is in truth: the fire of grace, the fire of pure and purifying love. This is the awesome judgement of humanity that I sometimes glimpse at nightfall, when I look into my heart.

RESURRECTION

And in my heart I see the city of the Holy Ghost arising from the flames of judgement; in my heart I see the New Jerusalem: immense and beautiful, twelve-walled, twelve-gated; its twelve holy gates admitting us into the twelve dimensions of the chakra of the heart; built round the fountain of the waters of life in the brain of the macrocosmos and expressed in individual men and women, my brothers and sisters, the children of light.

In dreams I walk among its colonnades, meeting friends remembered and unknown; all seems familiar, and yet astonishing and new. And when we converse, it is as though we are passing through cities inside one another: twelve-gated, majestic, astounding in their beauty: in their multiform gardens and parks and streets, in their towers and spires, their mansions and their terraces, their rivers and lakes and canals: at every step we encounter adventure; at every step we ask ourselves: 'How is it that from without a man is of such and such a height and such and such a volume, yet within he is limitless: there is no end to the love he can give and the love he can bear.'

In my heart, in the sea, in the blossoming almond trees, in the long-remembered image of a young girl of Bethsaida, in the words of my Master, Jesus, in the recollection of Mary Magdalene's humility and her love for Christ, in the thought of Mother Mary's kindliness abounding, in my heart I see the New Jerusalem and the children of light in its endless streets: their relationships of innocence and courtesy, their self-delighting spontaneity. I see between them a formality consistent with the laws of music, not restricting but expressing love; a decorum expediting love's polyphony.

I see in humanity's art, its games, its work, its discussions and arguments, its routines and sacraments, the symbolic displayed; I see the infinite appearing in the finite, the eternal in the transient.

And I see that whenever any moment in the New Jerusalem is opened, it is found to be limitless; one can enter into time as one can roam within a city: twelve-gated, immense: its streets the thoroughfares of paradise.

And I see in this New Jerusalem the Divine imagination pouring forth in every particle of every brick of every building, and men and women walking there, amazed at what unfolds before them, recollecting the past as one thinks of a dream.

And as the fig tree only offers figs or the lemon tree lemons, so I see the fruit of desire growing only on the tree of chastity.

And in the heart of the heart of the city, in the place of the fountain, I see the Advocate, the Counsellor, the Comforter, the Holy Spirit, the Mother, at once as simple as a child and unknowably mysterious; in her right hand a light like the sun and in her left hand a light like the moon, crowned with a crown of light: prismatic, awesome, fiery; her feet among the lotuses, while compassion streams forth from her eyes as she looks at the children who bathe her feet, and angels shout for joy.

All this I behold in my heart as though, as now, it is dusk or a short while after, and I am gazing at the outlines of a city on another hill, elusive in the darkness, an uncertain way away.

THE NAMES

And now as night falls—having first removed my shoes and placed my hands as Mary showed us, in Jerusalem at Pentecost—I recite this praise of Christ, affirming in a measured way, aloud:

'You are the Son of God, and I worship you.

'You are the Son of the Holy Spirit.

'You are her all-pervading Power personified.

'You were foretold by the Prophets.

'You were announced by the Angel Gabriel.

'You were conceived in your Mother's heart.

'You were born of a virgin.

'You are the eternal child.

'You are Ganesha.

'You are Kartikeya.

'You are Mahavishnu.

'You were born to Mary Mahalaxshmi.

'You were born at the darkest hour.

'You were born at *Diwali*.

'You were born in a stable, to show us humility.

'You were laid in a manger, in the dry straw of the world.

'The simple-hearted adored you.

'Lords Brahmadeva, Vishnu, and Shiva offered you frankincense, gold and myrrh.

'Your feet touched the heart of the world.

'You are beyond temptation.

'You turned water into wine.

'You walked on water.

'You baptised with the living waters of the Holy Spirit.

'You said, "He who is near me is near the fire."

'You came to cast a fire upon the world.

'You confounded the Scribes and denounced the Pharisees.

'You rejected all dogma.

'You cleansed the Temple of materialists.

'You cured the sick, you cast out demons, you gave eyes to the blind.

'You fed the hungry, you offered rest to the heavily-laden, you gave hope to the oppressed.

'You raised the dead.

'You said, "Blessed are those who know their need of God."

'You said, "Seek and you shall find."

'You said, "You must be born again."

'You preached the Gospel of the Kingdom of Heaven.

'You preached the forgiveness of sins.

'You commanded us to love one another.

'You absorb the *karma* of those who love you.

'The conditioning of those who love you, you dissolve.

'You are very kind.

'Love made you, Love bore you, Love wept over you, Love gloried in you.

'You bore the title, *Son of Man*.

'You are the eldest brother.

'You washed the feet of your disciples.

'You laid down your life for Mankind.

'You came to make us happy.

'In every way you sought to please your Mother.

'At every turn you glorified your Father.

'You said, "Cleave a piece of wood, and I am there. Lift up a stone: I am there." You exist in all things.

'You are holiness incarnate.

'You are infinite wisdom.

'You are the soul of generosity.

'You are the peacemaker.

'You are innocence: immaculate and absolute.

'You are the meaning of the universe.

'You are the essence of creation.

'You are the Word.

'You are the Logos.

'You are the Light of the World.

'You are the Way.

'You are the Door.

'You are the Good Shepherd.

'You are the Lamb of God.

'You are the True Vine.

'You are the Bread of Life.

'You are the Sun of righteousness.

'You are the Bright Morning Star.

'You are the Pantocrater, the Ruler.

'You are Salvator Mundi, the Saviour.

'You are the Amen, the *Omkara*.

'You are the Redeemer.

'You are the Messiah.

'You are the Alpha.

'You are the Omega.

'You are *Sahaja*.

'You are Emmanuel, and with those who love you always.

'You called forth a child and said, "Whoever humbles himself like this child is the greatest in the Kingdom of Heaven."

'You reside in the *Adi Agnya Chakra*, your abode is the palace of wisdom.

'You undertook the *tapasya* of creation.

'You submitted to be crucified, such is your love, your sense of duty, and your detachment.

'Those who crucified you, you forgave.

'When you were crucified, the curtain of the temple of organised religion was torn in two.

'It is said that you descended into hell and preached the Gospel to the damned, such is your compassion.

'On the third day you rose again.

'You are the Resurrection.

'You are Eternal Life.

'You are pure *chaitanya*.

'You showed that Truth is Love.

'You proved that Love is more powerful than evil.

'You proved that Love is stronger than death.

'You proved the Spirit's reality.

'You are he who comes again on the white horse of collective consciousness.

'You cannot accept impurities.

'You have eleven destructive powers.

'You are Sri Kalki.

'You carry a winnowing fork.

'You are the Lord of the Harvest.

'You are the Lord of the Last Judgement.

'You are awesome and invincible.

'You throw the evil-hearted and the lukewarm to the right and left.

'You are the Lord of the New Jerusalem.

'You are the support of the fruit of the Tree of Life.

'Where your attention moves, there move the great archangels, Gabriel and Michael.

'You promised the Comforter.

'Lord of Lords, we bow down to you!

'King of Kings, we salute you!

'Son of God, we adore you!

'You are the embodiment of your Mother's love.'

THE PRAYER

Then I turn to the Mother, the Holy Spirit, and make the following prayer—for a child should not be afraid to ask her for things, even though she may say, 'Not yet, not yet, but later.'

Come, most compassionate Mother,

Come, Queen of Earth and of Heaven,

Come: awaken, arise, and come forth

From your house, I beseech you.

With my attention I have woven

On the loom of my desire

A carpet patterned with sweet flowers,

With phoenixes and flowers,

With birds and fruit and flowers;

Its material: of dedication,

Its art: the ardour of my heart,

And its design: a Tree of Life,

And I have placed it on the way,

The narrow way within me,

On the central path within me,

That in comfort you may move towards

Your throne-room, holy Comforter.

So come forth, O come forth, I beseech you,

And be enthroned in my awareness,

Be enrobed in your robes of compassion,

And be crowned with your crown of bliss!

THE VOICE OF THE SEA

And now it is night in Ephesus, and I turn from the work of one day towards the morning of another. The boatmen sleep, and the quarrelsome gulls, and the priests in the Temple of Diana, and the masters and servants and slaves: every one of them sleeps, and even the whispers of the lovers in the pine groves above the beach have long since ceased. Only the nightingales and I are awake, the nightingales and I and the restless wind; and as one who meditates to music, so now I listen to the sea.

And this is my consolation in old age, I think: that the sea's voice is clearer at night than it is in the day. In the daytime the traffic of boats, the crying of gulls, the shouts of men, the disturbance of one's own incessant thinking obscures the sea's eternal resonance, but night dissolves the babel of the sunlit hours, the day's cacophony.

And likewise, now that night falls in my body's life, I hear the music of reality more lucidly than I could hear it in my youth, and the voices of my several selves which, in former days, demanded this, or wished for that, or petitioned for one thing and required another, have in the course of time grown silent.

The essential I perceive with more acuity, while the transient appears for what it is.

Therefore, when they ask my thoughts on this or that, or when they come for my advice, or when they fight among themselves, or when they speculate about the nature of the Absolute, I no longer care to counsel them.

We also bothered Christ with trivialities when I was young, but he would say: 'Forget those things which trouble you and seek but the Kingdom of God, for when that is found, you will look and say, "My troubles are resolved."'

And: 'Seek the Kingdom in all innocence, for you must attain your meaning, you must know what joy is yours.'

THE SPIRIT

And now, as night falls in my life, the sense that there is something inextinguishable within us comes to me and grows in me, like the smile that grows on a young mother's face as she watches her child at play among the olive trees, unaware of her watching him.

It grows and grows within me, this recognition, like the smile on a mother's face made the lovelier because the one at whom she gazes does not sense her being there, perceiving him with love.

There is something permanent within us which neither time nor sorrow nor death nor evil can ever extinguish.

What is it?

It is the Spirit, which watches.

It watches and waits; it watches, it loves.

Whom does it watch?

It watches us.

What does it see?

It sees everything.

It is God's attention in the heart.

It is what we really are.

It sees our striving, our worries, our hatreds, our passion, our birth in a lightened room and our dying in a darkened one, alone, while beyond the shutters the business of another day goes by. It sees our striving and our failings, our pettiness, our moments of nobility. It loves us.

It is us, yet we are not it. No, we hide in our striving, our doing, our wanting, our thinking, our feeling, our sleeping. We are lost in these things, like a child who has wandered from his parents' garden to the city streets . . . and round and round he goes, now to the left side, now to the right, lured by the future and impelled by the past, into a maze of lanes and alleys, on labyrinthine roads unending.

And round and round he goes, until he forgets his home, his parents and his name itself. He is fostered by others, assumes a new identity, grows conditioned by his habits and reactions and the patterns of his culture, becomes a stranger to himself.

Such is our position in the world. We have put on the garments of space and time, we are born and live and die, and then again we take our birth, and we desire and strive and suffer, not knowing what we are in truth.

And though we may say that we *think* or we *feel* we are the Spirit, or pay due respect to the Spirit, or reinterpret what the Spirit means—or doubt it, or deny it—still we have not yet *become* it. And that we should become it was the aim and end of all Christ's labours in this world.

And so, as night falls in my life and the sense of something inextinguishable and beautiful again grows within me, I know that what I used to fear: that the work of our Lord would prove to have been in vain: will not now happen and cannot happen. Let Paul and his kind build Church after Church, but still it cannot happen. Let them build their Christianity out of power and fear, not truth and awe, but still it cannot happen. Let them grant their mock baptisms, let them invent a dogma, let them organise a priesthood, but it cannot happen. Let them neglect the Holy Spirit and forget their Mother, but it cannot happen. Let the reasoners, in all their ignorance and arrogance, repudiate the Spirit, but it cannot happen. Let them say that black is white or both are grey, but it will not happen. Let them reject or distort the words of Jesus, but it will not happen.

And the reason that it will not happen? Because the unreal is at last without foundation; when the cool, fresh wind of God's compassion blows throughout our beings, it will be dissolved as if it were a dream.

SILENCE

And now as night falls gently in my life, I look back on what I have written and feel the insufficiency of it.

And yet, what else could I have said? Or should I have bequeathed to my friends only silence: only silence and light and a token of love, and a heartfelt recommendation.

For these days in my meditations it is as though I am saying to Jesus: 'When I think of you, I cannot think of you; a silence engulfs me.

'And when I remember you, I remember light: light irradiates me.

'And when I repeat your name, in my heart it is *love* that my lips pronounce.

'And if I try to describe you, I cannot describe you; so many are your aspects, no words can do you justice. Yet if I had to choose one word to accord you, it would be that one which means innate, essential, spontaneous, innocent, alive, and undeterred by any obstacles whatsoever: it would be the word *sahaja*.

'And if I call to mind your teachings, then out of all of them one invitation—or command—stands out, one testament that I would leave to this afflicted world in its confusion: one admonition and appeal: one simple saying that you gave to me:

'"O child: behold thy Mother."'

AFTERWORD

So ends this book which might have been written by John, near death in Ephesus. But is it true, or in what way is it true?

When a musician plays the music of the past, he may not play it exactly as the composer first performed it or envisaged it being performed, but his execution may yet be beautiful and powerful, it may nevertheless have such significance for us that we can say, yes, his playing is true and what he is playing has truth.

Here I have tried to be like that musician.

But—it might be asked—from where does this music come?

It comes from a reading of the Gospels, of the Acts of John and of Thomas, of the Infancy Gospel of Thomas, of some of the Gnostic books and the *agrapha* of Christ. It comes from logic, and it comes from meditation.

And if it is asked on what authority this work is based?

I can only say that it is based on my own self-knowledge, which was given to me by Shri Mataji Nirmala Devi. It was given freely and spontaneously, and verifiably, just as it is given to all who desire it, through her work of *Sahaja Yoga*.

What, then, is Sahaja Yoga, and who is Shri Mataji? The answers to these questions are in a way to be found in this book, I believe—but I cannot impose them, nor do I wish to impose them, on others. I simply offer those answers in the form of *Sophia* itself.

So, here I have tried to be like that musician who knows very well that some among his audience will not care much for what he plays, and that others may question his musicianship, and that others may only half-listen—yet who trusts that there may be some who, forgiving his infelicities, will give their awareness to him in the form of receptivity as he gives his to them in the form of artistry, and who will comprehend his music in their hearts.

Now the work is finished and the musician prepares to retire, his business complete. He stands and bows within himself to Jesus, our Lord, the Son of Man, the very image of the Spirit and the meaning of Creation. He bows to Shri Mataji Nirmala Devi, whose measureless, enlightening compassion, so he feels, goes out to all the world. And, lastly, he offers his music to the seekers of truth.

Printed in Great Britain
by Amazon